LORD,
WHY ME!

LORD, WHY ME!

by
Elizabeth Gardner

All Scripture quotations are taken from the King James Version unless noted as TLB (*The Living Bible*) or "paraphrased," meaning the author's paraphrase has been used.

Dedication

To the exalted Savior, Jesus Christ our Lord

And affectionately dedicated to

Frank, Jeffery, and Renee,
who are in the glory of His presence,
clothed with celestial grace.

Acknowledgments

My deepest appreciation to Dr. T.N. Seshagiri, who not only rendered medical attention to my dear ones, but also took his valuable time to give medical-technical data and explanations for this book. My thanks to Geno Lawrenzi whose support and writing abilities gave me encouragement to complete this manuscript; and to David Molina for his suggestions and his help with the editing of sections of the book. I also want to acknowledge my precious husband, Rick, for his kindness and love. Through his patient and understanding heart, I have drawn much more than strength.

Introduction

The kites were mere specks in the sky, dots against a blue horizon. From the patio door, I could see Frank running alongside Jeff and Renee, trying to get the kites even higher. I had to laugh at my husband's excitement. He was almost as enthusiastic about kite flying as the children.

Renee was smiling and hurrying to keep stride with her daddy. Her cheeks were flushed with excitement. Jeff, who had just turned six, displayed an air of confidence in his sport; after all, he was the "man" in the family. In Jeff's eyes, Renee was just a little sister who kept getting in the way. What was most important to me was that they were having fun—good, clean, wholesome fun. We were a family and that meant everything to me.

Frank was a good husband, faithful and hard working. I tried to be the perfect partner by keeping a clean house, saving money, and by making sure my family stayed healthy and happy.

We were living in northeastern Ohio in a place I had

dreamed about all my life—a brown, brick home in the country.

It was a perfect setting for a happy marriage, and I had no complaints. Except—except the roast was burning!

I ran into the kitchen and managed to get it out just in time. Then I returned to the door to watch my husband and children at play before calling them in to have their dinner. Kite flying was a favorite sport in our part of Ohio. It was good exercise for the children and Frank, and I sometimes joined them in the fun.

Sometimes things are frozen in your mind. You can remember the way a favorite aunt looked in a photo, or the way you wore a silly hat to a picnic when you were twelve. As the kites ascended, I watched Renee's long blonde hair gliding through the air as she ran beside Jeff. He was smiling, and as he caught up with Frank, a Polaroid picture was imprinted in my mind. It was a picture that would last a lifetime. It would be the last time the children would be in the same picture with their father—the last time my heart would be filled with the excitement and joy of watching my family share happy times together.

"Time to eat," I yelled. Frank heard me and signaled that they were coming. He let the children reel in the kites, and the colorful bits of paper and long Chinese tails came crashing to the green Ohio countryside.

As my three companions entered the door one by one, I could see how the excitement of kite flying was still filling their souls.

Between bites of food, Jeff told how high his kite had flown. At the same time, Renee chimed in with, "Mine was even higher!" Frank finally settled the argument. Yes, his was the highest of all.

After dinner, we all sat down to watch a Charlie Brown TV special.

Bedtime followed. Frank picked Jeff up on his shoulders, while I attempted to do the same with Renee. Finally, as I succeeded, like soldiers, we marched to bed and tucked them in their beds with lots of kisses and goodnight farewells.

And so another day had passed. A day filled with good family fun, sharing memorable moments together. A day perhaps that is common to many American families throughout the country.

There was something I didn't know. Had I known it, I wouldn't have gone to sleep that night feeling carefree, happy, content and secure in my home.

Within three short years, all three of them—Frank, Renee, and then Jeff—would be dead.

Chapter 1

I grew up in the hilly town of Braddock Hills, a lovely suburb of Pittsburgh. Braddock Hills has a friendly rural population of around twenty-five hundred people. It's a tight-knit community, where everybody knows everyone else.

My parents were devout Catholics and raised me in the Catholic tradition. Even though I had to walk ten miles round-trip, I went to Mass every Sunday. As a family we attended all the feast days, and were faithful during the Lenten season in going to the Stations of the Cross every Friday. I enjoyed catechism classes, which taught us about God and all the Catholic beliefs.

I was thrilled by my First Holy Communion. Dressed in white, and feeling quite saintly, I thought I was one of the holiest creatures in all the world. I had taken my first step toward God.

At the age of eleven, I received my Confirmation, which meant I confirmed my faith in the church.

The only spiritual knowledge I had came from the Catholic church. In those days we were taught it was the only true church, and to attend any other was forbidden.

My childhood was filled with simplicity and fun. My friends and I swung on homemade swings. We jumped rope, played jacks, practiced somersaults, and rode bikes from morning till night. Some evenings, we would go for walks up to the cemetery near our hill. Two of my closest friends had lost their mother. We would pack a lunch and walk up to her grave, which was on top of the highest hill of the cemetery. Along the way we would pick wildflowers to put on her grave and offer a prayer for her soul.

Living in the suburbs brought our young lives some down-to-earth entertainment. "Hide-and-go-seek" and "Simon says" were at the top of our list. Often, especially at the end of summer and beginning of fall, we spent many evenings sitting around a fire roasting fresh-picked corn from one of the neighbors' gardens. We sang songs like "One Hundred Bottles of Beer on the Wall" and rounds of "Row, Row, Row Your Boat."

Baseball and football were my favorites. Being the only girl on the team, I made sure I played just as well as the boys. My parents were amazed on each occasion when the boys came pounding on the door with their gloves in their hands, calling me to come and play ball. I guess that's why, when I was eight years old, it was so natural for them to buy me a football suit for Christmas instead of a doll. I felt I could measure up to my older brother in any sandlot game.

Larry was three years older than I, and I resented all three years. He received all the privileges, while I was always told, "You are too young." My parents' attention always seemed to be centered on him. Subconsciously, I reacted by developing a tom-boyish atti-

2

tude that lasted till I was eleven years old, at which time my newborn brother appeared to rid me of this characteristic. Playing mommy to Conrad helped to develop in me a more feminine outlook in my young life. Ball games soon became secondary and began to give way to a more normal realm for a pre-teen girl. I began dreaming of the time I would have my own children. I was so attached to my brother, I took him everywhere I went. My dates especially enjoyed my little brother when he accompanied us to the movies.

One of my most interesting adult friends was Mr. Lewis, a black man who ran our small variety store. It had been converted from an old garage and was a gathering place for the kids of the community. Mr. Lewis had a warm personality and always seemed to have time for a small girl who asked questions. I remember he kept his big black Bible placed within easy reach on the counter. I often wondered what was so interesting in that big black book he was reading every time I came into the store. I asked him one day what he was reading and he told me about Moses, the children of Israel and many other children's Bible stories. Before I would leave, he would hand me a popsicle. I had almost wished we weren't Catholic so we could own a book like Mr. Lewis's.

When winter would come, we would pull our sleds to a nearby hill. The hill was always packed with young people. We would exhale to make "smoke" in the frosty air. Another thing that was to strike me later was the lack of prejudice in our little corner of the world. Black and white youngsters alike would share the hill. Racial bias was just not part of our perspective. The competition was fierce, though, as we would try to set speed records going down hill, then huff and puff to see who could get up to the crest first for another slide down.

Essentially, those pre-puberty years were ideal ones from certain viewpoints. If I had any regrets, it was that I felt I was not the recipient of as much attention as I yearned for. In retrospect, I believe the fact that I was a middle child, between two brothers, had a lot to do with the insecurities I experienced at that age.

A new era was dawning for me. As I grew into the teen years, I found my interests changing from sledding, hop-scotch and jacks to sock hops, football games, and Cokes at the corner drugstore.

And dates.

The single most significant event of my teens came at sixteen when I encountered my "first love." More appropriately, though, I would have to say "first loves," in the plural, because there were two young men who entered this crucial period of my life.

The first half of this "first love" was Wayne Wallis, a fun-loving, kindly young man I met during my sophomore year in high school. Two years older than I, Wayne had hazel eyes, wavy brown hair and a charming smile. It was easy to be attracted to him and the fact that he found me attractive flattered me, since I was still quite introverted. A few months later I was to meet the second half of this "first love." Harry McFarland, a star center on the football team that went to the regional championships that year, was Wayne's best friend.

Although physically different, two people couldn't have been so alike inwardly had they been born identical twins. Wayne and "Bubby," as Harry was affectionately called by his friends, had virtually identical personality characteristics. Both were gentle, considerate, understanding and made me feel a sense

4

of belonging, of self-worth. The one striking difference between the two was that Bubby's emotions ran deeper than Wayne's. Bubby more easily expressed his sensitivities, whereas I had the impression that Wayne had a tendency to sometimes hide his real feelings.

To any other young lady, this situation might sound ideal. But in my case, it became a traumatic experience, leading to confusion and a spiritual upheaval that was to later affect my adult life.

I maintained my moral values through it all. It wasn't like I was dating both at the same time. I'd been dating Wayne when, through a quirk of events, I got to know Bubby. It was awhile after some soul-searching that I decided it was Bubby with whom I felt more comfortable, or so I thought at the time. At that time I was not aware of the reasons why I preferred one or the other. Later I went back to Wayne, then back to Bubby. In looking back, I realized that I was in fact hungry for love and acceptance, and so whichever one would give me the most attention and affection would receive my considerations. It was not like it was puppy love or simple infatuations; they were mature, reasoned-out relationships, and at certain points I did discuss marriage with each one of them.

First and foremost, I wanted a perfect marriage. I had seen too many marriages go awry, even in my own family. I had seen rocky unions, some of which hung together only by a thin strand. I did not want that for myself and my future mate, whoever that would be. I steadfastly adhered to the belief that God was, is and will be the head of all creation. God came first in all things, and if a marriage was based on this tenet, then it couldn't help but be a perfect one.

During this period I was fortified by the teachings

from the catechism on the holiness of God. The words, "Be holy, for I am holy," stayed with me as a guiding light in these relationships. More importantly, I wanted to be chaste on my wedding day.

The devil seems to work overtime at trying to impress young people. Yes, there were temptations for us, but to this day, I remain thankful for those early moral teachings and for the fact that both Wayne and Bubby were respectful young men. Looking back, I'm sure that there were some frustrations, but God, love, and respect saw us through. My prayer was, "God, if I keep myself pure and chaste, you will grant me a good marriage."

Indeed I prayed that I would make the right choice between Wayne and Bubby. But a decision was not to come and this led me to further frustrations. At length, I prayed that God in His mercy would rid me of both of them, perhaps so that I would not have to make a decision.

The trauma came not in trying to decide between two people, two gentlemen, whom I truly esteemed and loved. Rather, the anguish came from my search to determine whether it was possible to love two people simultaneously. Perhaps I wanted not to hurt either of them.

I began making weekly pilgrimages to the church on Saturdays for confession and a period of prayerful meditation in the way the nuns had taught me. The prayers consisted of saying the rosary. Yet I felt that a repetitive prayer was not sufficient, so sometimes, I would kneel before the crucifix at the altar and have a conversation with God. Seeking further help in my dilemma, I enlisted the help of my parish priest, Father Berg, a kind, elderly man who I felt could give me some enlightenment. He reminded me of Mr. Lewis, both elderly and pious in appearance. Father Berg, perhaps not fully understanding my problem, or perhaps it was that I could not fully communicate the scope of it to him, did little to soothe my troubled soul. I had wanted to hear things from the Bible as I had remembered Mr. Lewis telling me. But most of the time, Father Berg would talk about sports, school, or my latest date—in short, everything except what I wanted to hear. I confess too that I was embarrassed to ask him specific questions about what was really on my mind. And so I would go home empty-handed, still in search of an answer.

While I was expecting a great revelation, unbeknownst to me, God was working for me behind the scenes. In a sense, my prayers were being answered all the time because God often works in mysterious ways. However, I did not realize it at the time.

Bubby and I graduated in 1961, after which he joined the U.S. Army Reserves and went off for six months of training. Eventually, Wayne began receding into the background and Bubby withdrew when he became perplexed over my insecurities and indecisions.

Despite the fact that these two young men were now a part of a closed chapter, I felt some relief. I felt that if I was to come to understand myself and what part I was to play in this world, it would manifest itself through a future act of God.

One other significant event occurred during this latter part of my teens. In March of the year I graduated, another prayer had been answered for me. I was eighteen when an unspoken wish I'd harbored for many years came true: a baby sister was born. I'd felt all this time that if I had a younger sister I would have someone to relate to. But it was too late for me to realize any personal fulfillment from her presence—so I thought. Later in life, she became extremely close to me and shared the same love of Jesus Christ that I found a few years later.

Andrea was born with a rare disease that left her with two hundred and fifty bone fractures at birth. Her doctor gave her only three days at the most to live. I wanted my sister to live; in a sense, I needed her. For the first time in my young life, I dared venture outside the Catholic church for help.

I'd heard about the evangelist Kathryn Kuhlman through a neighbor. I'd heard about the miracles and healings that were taking place through her, and wondered if she could perform what would certainly amount to a miracle in the life of my baby sister. I wrote to the evangelist and asked for her prayers, even though I knew it was forbidden, according to the teachings of my church. My sister lived, and to this day, although confined to a wheelchair, she continues to be an inspiration not only to me, but to others. Her love for Jesus Christ and abundant faith in Him to see her through this life touches many hearts. As she shares the saving grace of His love with others, many souls are won to Him. She tells them, "I found Jesus where I'm at, and you can find Him where you are."

When I think of Andrea, I realize that a miracle spared her life that March of 1961.

If the situation with Wayne and Bubby had kept me in close contact with the Creator, then the crisis over Andrea had reinforced my faith in God. But more than that, the crisis also served to heighten my yearnings to get to know God better. Indeed, this was to have a bearing on the next steppingstone in life.

A period of semi-tranquility surrounded me shortly after my nineteenth birthday. No longer was the Wayne-Buddy situation hovering over my head. Andrea had survived and I had gone to work. My family moved to Ohio and I stayed behind in the family home. This afforded me time to sort out my life, to try to set my sights.

I wanted a closer union with God. I thought of the evangelist Kathryn Kuhlman, of the nuns who had given me my early teachings about Christ. And I thought about priests. Evangelists, priests, and nuns, I deduced, must have an inside track to God. More and more I was beginning to lean toward a life in the clergy. I realized I couldn't be an evangelist, for I was a Catholic. I couldn't be a priest, since only men are priests. Realistically, that left but one choice: to become a nun.

It was settled then; a spiritual life would be the one for me. That's where I'd find my true happiness, I thought. Now came another decision to make: what order? I considered being a teaching sister, but that would involve years in college. Then I thought about becoming a nursing nun. This didn't appeal to me. I thought of the needs of the world, and ultimately it was this trend of thought that led me to a decision. I felt that what the world needed most in those difficult days was prayer. I would become a cloistered nun.

My father was especially concerned when I told him I was thinking of entering the Carmelite order.

"If you get into that group, we'll never see you again," he persisted. "They only let families come in on special days. It's just like being in jail."

Although my mother tended to agree with him, she wasn't as vocal in her objections. One person who sided with me was Keith, a maintenance worker at a local hospital. I met him during a week's stay at the hospital after suffering intestinal pains. Keith was washing windows when we started talking about life in general. The conversation switched around to religion, and Keith remarked that he had just left the monastery.

I was fascinated. Finally I had met someone my own age who could tell me something about the church and its mysteries. He was only too eager to share with me some of the things he had learned in the monastery.

He described in detail his prayer life, the silence that pervaded the building, and how a person could get closer to God. When he talked about the love everyone felt for each other, I knew I had found my calling.

We decided that the world was, as Keith put it, "in chaos." The world needed prayer for peace. Dedicating myself to my mission, I would simply get lost in the Carmelite order and find peace and happiness—and God. I felt like Joan of Arc.

I made a telephone call to the order's office in Pittsburgh and informed the mother superior I wanted to become a nun.

Briskly, she listed what I would need. It was necessary that I have a letter of recommendation from the parish priest. This would permit me to become an outsister. The term meant I wouldn't be an official part of the cloistered order until I took my solemn vows. When the sisters were convinced this was what I really wanted, and that I was ready, I would become a member of the order.

The thought of becoming a nun filled me with excitement, along with a touch of fear. There was so much I didn't know. My parents were still reluctant to accept the idea, but Keith gave me the encouragement I needed. On the drive from our home to the convent, Keith came along.

With only the clothes on my back and some personal items, we rode along Route 30. I looked at the trees in bloom and the pale Pennsylvania sky and tried to relax, but it was hard. As if he knew what I was feeling, Keith gave my hand a squeeze of encouragement.

The convent was in a tranquil setting, surrounded by tall shade trees and flower gardens. High walls concealed the inner buildings from the curious. The walls were covered with vines and reminded me of a college campus rather than a convent. It was altogether lovely.

Sister Mary Ellen, a young nun wearing a floor-length brown habit, welcomed me with a smile.

"We are glad to have you here, Betty," she said. We followed her into the open foyer.

"Please be seated," she said graciously. "Mother Superior will be with you shortly." Although she was friendly and open, she acted as though she was used to being obeyed. We remained seated, waiting nervously for the arrival of Mother Superior.

But Sister Mary Ellen wasn't finished.

Gently, but firmly, she said, "You'll have to say good-bye to your family, Betty. Now is the time."

I turned toward my parents. Keith looked at me expectantly. So many things raced through my mind, but I couldn't tell them what I felt. I hugged Keith and my parents. Then I turned to the sister.

"I'm ready," I said simply.

It's hard to describe the feeling I had when my only contact with the outside world disappeared and the doors slammed shut. I felt alone, yet I was filled with anticipation; something good—no, something great—

was going to happen.

But, where was Mother Superior?

A voice came out of the darkness. She was in the room with me, but hidden behind a large screen. During my entire stay in the convent, I would never see her face.

She welcomed me to the order and told me that I would soon be receiving my habit. As she spoke, I felt strange. I wanted to see what she looked like, to feel her hand on my head. Instead, this voice that floated out of nowhere was giving me instructions designed to change my life.

"Prayer is an important part of our life at the convent, Betty," she declared. "It will begin at 4:00 AM daily. Do not have any contact with the outside world for the next six months. No telephone calls, no newspapers, no visitors. Do you understand?"

I nodded.

"If you have any questions, Sister Mary Ellen will help you. That is all."

As quickly as she had appeared, the voice and Mother Superior were gone. I heard her shoes tap-tapping down the hallway. Somehow, I felt as though another door had been closed.

My new world in the convent was one of silence. Normally a person interested in everything around me, I was reduced to being a solitary figure who communicated with no one. It didn't really bother me much. I was in the convent to learn about God, not to let the world know how clever I could be. So what if I had to exist in a tiny cellular room? If I could increase my knowledge of God and walk with Him in such a place, it was a small sacrifice.

The day began at 4:00 AM with two hours of reading

from the prayer book. I would repeat the prayers over and over again. We didn't study the Bible. In fact, there were few references to the Bible, the convent preferring to lead us in its own method of instruction.

Since my own knowledge of the Bible was quite limited, this had little effect on me. Later the Lord would begin to deal with me about this phase of my spiritual education.

Mass began at 6:00 A.M. The voices of the already cloistered nuns, chanting prayers in Latin, were beautiful and moving to a novice out-sister. I could literally lose myself in the prayers and forget I existed. There was very little of me for the world to see. I was covered from head to foot with the habit. Even my hands were covered by my brown uniform. Talking or fellowship with the other nuns was forbidden except for a daily twenty-minute period during which we could speak. When the time came to communicate, we found we had little to say. We might talk about whether it was going to rain, or discuss what we had sold in the small chapel gift shop that day. After a few ill-fated attempts at conversation, I gave up and went to my room to "communicate."

When I entered the convent, I had to give up all my "worldly" things. Under the rules, I was permitted to keep only the clothes I wore. The program was designed to eliminate self and focus on spiritual things. Our food was limited to plain fare—mostly bread and water, with meat served once a week. For breakfast we received toast, cereal, and coffee. It was definitely a diet geared for weight control.

As an out-sister, I was expected to remain a year. At the end of my apprenticeship, the mother superior would determine if I was cut out to stand such a life of deprivation and discipline.

Our day's schedule went like this: prayer, 4:00 to 6:00 AM; chapel, 6:00 to 7:00 AM; breakfast; then we did our chores the rest of the day. Dinner was served at 6:00 PM, and prayer at 7:00 PM would end the day.

We had half an hour to tidy up our rooms or to take care of other minor chores before 10:00 PM lights out. Our other daily responsibilities included making sandals, cleaning our rooms, doing chores around the convent, and working in the gift shop.

In silence, a sister would hand me a mop and pail of water. In silence, I would scrub the floor until I could see my reflection. When I was through, another job would be assigned to me. There were no words of praise or small talk, no "Nice job, Betty." I could have been born without ears for all the good they did me.

It didn't take long before the doubts began. I started asking myself, "What am I doing here?"

I wasn't achieving the goal I had set for myself. I was no more spiritual than I had been when I entered the convent. I didn't know any more about God than I did before. Inside, I felt empty, yearning for a closeness to God that just wasn't there. As far as the outside world was concerned, Betty Ann Yeager had ceased to exist.

I liked the convent. There was a kind of love and closeness between the sisters that even the imposed wall of silence couldn't separate. And yet, somehow, I knew God had a different path for me to follow. I prayed for God to show me the way. My mind was whirling with indecisions I thought I had left behind. Would peace ever come to me?

One day during prayer in the chapel, I became violently ill. I got up and hurried to the bathroom where I vomited repeatedly. The other nuns became concerned

14

and notified Mother Superior, who ordered me to bed.

I stayed, isolated, in my bed for four days. The sisters slid my food to me through a slit in the wall. Because I was so sick, I ate very little. My physical condition quickly deteriorated and I lost weight. It seemed I would never stop throwing up.

As I lay there wondering what was wrong with me, Sister Mary Ellen entered the room. She handed me a note from the mother superior.

"I'm sorry, Betty," she said.

The note informed me that I would have to leave the convent. I needed medical help, and the convent simply wasn't equipped to provide me with it.

When I was better, she would discuss my future with me.

Although I realized I needed a doctor, I still wanted to be a nun—or did I? I called Wayne and asked him if he would come by and give me a ride home. I left the convent with mixed emotions.

I was so weak, I could barely get out of bed without help. But something happened. As we drove out the convent drive, it seemed as if I felt a little better. Driving down the highway my stomach began to settle. The closer we got to my home, or maybe it was the farther we got from the convent, the better I felt. Had God allowed this sickness to come upon me so I would leave the convent, I wondered. Knowing my insecurities, He knew what would have to take place for me to move.

My parents had moved to Ohio, so Wayne suggested I come stay with him and his grandmother till I was on my feet again. His grandmother, a wonderfully wise old woman, nursed me back to health. Within days I felt like myself again.

Wayne's grandmother—I called her Gram—was a stern, down-to-earth person.

"You did good to get out of that convent," she said. "You don't need that kind of life!" I respected her feelings and her firm convictions and I listened with interest to her comments.

She had many wise sayings and understandings about life in general. Since I was a captive audience, she piled them onto me.

After two weeks, I felt I was completely recovered. What should I do? Maybe if I saw my parents, I could decide if I wanted to return to the convent. So I said goodbye to Wayne and his grandmother, and booked passage on a train to Canton, Ohio.

Chapter 2

"Hey, Betty Ann's here," Dad shouted as I walked through the door. My parents were glad to see me, although my mother, staying in character, was more restrained in her welcome. While I recuperated fully, they treated me like a guest. Life was back to normal in the Yeager household.

Dad had a job as warehouse manager for a seed company. I was twenty and blossoming into an attractive young woman. And one day, as simple as that, I knew I wouldn't be returning to the convent.

Dad wanted me to date. He had a friend he wanted me to meet whose nickname was "Chicken." In many ways, some of them not very subtle, Dad kept telling me what a great guy this Chicken was. He worked as a mechanic at a service station up the street.

"You ought to meet this guy," Dad said after Chicken had repaired our 1961 Rambler. "This kid is the best mechanic in town. He has a car with a four-speed on the floor. Drag races with it too and has won a lot of trophies."

I smiled. "Do they call him Chicken because he has a scrawny neck?"

"No," said Dad, grinning. "Because he lays eggs." But he continued to praise Chicken every chance he got. One day I agreed to meet this hot rodder with the unusual name.

Chicken's real name was Frank Self. Unlike the other young men in town, he didn't push himself on people. Frank was a quiet, sensitive person with a good sense of humor. He didn't have much confidence in himself, but I liked him right away, although I didn't let him know it.

Purposely ignoring Frank, I turned to the owner of the service station and said, "What do you people do in this town for excitement?" I hoped Frank was listening.

Smoke Moffit smiled and nodded to Frank.

"Here's a guy who can show you a good time. Hey, Chicken, tell this young lady where she can go to have fun." He roared with laughter while Frank turned a deep crimson.

Frank was tall and slender with straw-colored hair and big blue eyes. Although he was twenty-one, he didn't date. His only love in life was cars. If there was anyone in Canton more innocent than I was, it had to be him.

Ignoring me, Frank walked into the next room where several young men were talking. Smoke asked him to run down the road and get him something to eat, since it was lunchtime.

Frank surprised me by asking if he could use my car.

"Just take care of it," I said reluctantly.

The restaurant was a block away. Frank returned

18

almost immediately with cheeseburgers and French fries.

As he handed me my keys, I decided to take the aggressive approach.

"Why do they call you Chicken?"

He blushed. It was one of his most endearing characteristics.

"Aw, I lived in the country most of my life," he explained with a shrug. "Worked on a farm and helped support the family after my father died. Anyhow, the kids started calling me Chicken because I used to feed the chickens. The name stuck, I guess."

Deciding I liked him and felt sorry for him at the same time, I became bolder.

"You drove my car," I said. "Now it's my turn to drive your car."

With a grin, he tossed me the keys. "There they are. Think you can handle it? It's four-speed."

In answer, I started the engine, gunned the motor, and peeled off down the street. When I got back, Frank was scratching his head sheepishly and his friends were laughing.

"You're really something," he said. Instantly we were attracted to each other, and the two of us were hooked.

Frank looked at me and asked if I wanted to take a ride.

"You're not afraid, are you?" he added.

"No," I answered with a calmness I didn't really feel. But my heart was racing. What did he plan to do?

He threw open the door on the passenger's side and I got in. Frank got behind the wheel and took off, sending a shower of gravel rattling the pavement behind us.

The speedometer crept up—50, 60, 70. Frank turned onto a country road and the houses fell behind us. When the needle hit 100, he kept it there. Once he looked at me, I looked back, courageously, I hoped. After a moment or two, Frank slowed to the legal speed limit. I had passed the test.

When we got back to the station, I didn't want him to leave, so I invited him for a ride in my car. We drove and talked about everything—his family, my family, school, and God. Hours passed and we somehow managed to burn up two tanks of gas. By the time I got home, it was four in the morning. I couldn't believe it.

My parents were waiting up for me, as I had expected. They were concerned, knowing I didn't know anyone in town. "Where have you been?" my dad demanded.

"With Chicken," I said calmly, munching an apple.

Dad smiled. If I had told him I had won a million dollars, he couldn't have been happier. They told me goodnight and I ran up to bed, giddy with the stirrings of love, youth and a beautiful harvest moon.

We started dating. Three weeks later, it seemed the most natural thing in the world when I asked Frank to marry me.

I had just passed my twenty-first birthday. Frank was extremely shy. The only thing he could talk about comfortably was cars. I loved him and felt he would make a good husband. Since he was obviously too shy to tell me how he felt, I decided to charge ahead. One night we went to an ice cream parlor for a sundae.

Before I took two bites of dessert, Frank knew this was to be no ordinary evening.

"Sonny," I said demurely, using the nickname his family selected for him, "I love you."

Frank gulped and turned red. But he responded the way I hoped he would.

"Me too," he said.

While the soda jerk was making out our bill, I said softly, "I think I'd like to be married to you."

There was silence. Frank finally said, "Me too," and he kissed me. Bells were going off, rockets were exploding, but the soda jerk didn't hear a thing. He handed Frank the bill and said, "That'll be sixty cents, please."

In May we announced our engagement, and planned an October wedding. Frank didn't attend any church. Of course I wanted him to become Catholic, but I wanted that to be his decision. One Sunday I was on my way to Mass, when he stopped by to visit. When I told him where I was going, he asked if he could accompany me. My heart leaped, but I did my best to hold my composure. "Sure," I said, "let's go."

This was the first time he had ever been in a Catholic church. I knew by his reaction that it was very strange to him. He sat in his seat during the whole Mass and just watched and listened. On our way home, he asked me a million questions. The one thing that bothered him the most was all the statues of Mary, Joseph, and Francis of Assisi. I explained to him how very important they were. "Mary was Jesus' mother, and very close to him. We petition her and she goes to her Son and asks Him for us. Because He loves her so much, He will grant our requests through her. Joseph, being His stepfather, is also respected and petitioned."

Frank said nothing, and I didn't want to confuse him any more than he had already been. He began to attend church with me every Sunday. On one occasion, after Mass, he told me he had gone to see the priest to start classes to become a Catholic. I was surprised at his announcement, and delighted. He attended the classes faithfully. When it came time for him to baptized, he asked my father if he would stand for him. Frank had become very fond of my father and vice versa. My father was pleased he had considered him for the honor.

October approached very quickly, and our wedding day had arrived. The ceremony drew more than one hundred and fifty friends and relatives to St. Joan of Arc Church. My father handed me to Frank, and I stepped up to the altar alongside of him; then we began to walk the few steps up to where the priest was waiting. I realized for the first time I was walking up to a new beginning of my life, a life of sharing and caring for someone else. I wanted so much to fulfill this responsibility God was giving me.

At the reception that evening, the joy of a marriage feast was in the air. The band played the happy tunes of our traditional Slovakian polka music. Sounds of laughter and jubilant dancing filled the room. After the food and refreshments were served, the traditional cutting of the cake began, and as Frank shoved the cake in my mouth and kissed me, I felt totally happy for the first time in my life. The Carmelite order was as far from me as the South Pole is from the North.

We were so excited over the little cottage we rented in the country, we decided to spend our wedding night there. The next morning we set out for our honeymoon at the lake.

Frank grew quickly in his newly adopted faith, and became as involved in the church as I was. Like me, Frank was searching for meaning in his spiritual life. We attended Mass faithfully together, and felt we couldn't be happier with our church and our lives together.

We loved our home, even if somebody else did own it. I was determined to make Frank a good wife and labored long hours to keep the house clean and to have scrumptious hot meals on the table when he came home from work.

Two years after we were married, we built a brown, brick home out in the country that Frank so loved. Along with our new home, God blessed us with a son, whom we named Jeffery. He had blond hair and blue eyes, just like his daddy.

When the nurse carried my son in to me and I felt the small warm bundle against my breast, I gave God a silent word of thanks. I had always dreamed of having a little boy with blue eyes and blond hair.

Jeff had a rather sickly childhood, almost from the time I brought him home from the hospital. He had a stomach problem at the age of nine weeks, and required emergency surgery because of a malfunctioning pyloric valve. The surgeon said an operation was necessary to open the valve so food could be admitted to the stomach. We were grateful when the two-hour operation turned out to be successful. He was stricken with allergies at birth. The older he became, the worse the allergies. He developed asthma and had to be taken to the hospital several times. There were many times my heart ached because of his difficulty in breathing.

After he suffered through a rash of severe asthma attacks, our doctor suggested I take him to an allergy specialist. Jeff was admitted to Akron Children's Hospital.

The doctor tested him and told us we would have to give up our apricot-colored poodle, whom Jeff loved so very much. The tests showed she had been one of the guilty culprits in triggering his bronchial attacks.

Jeff was only three. I thought he would never stop crying when we got rid of Suzi. From that day on, Jeff's attacks were much less severe. With the allergy shots prescribed by the doctor, and our lovable little dog gone, my son's health improved considerably.

Jeff grew into a loving little boy with a very kind heart, which he so beautifully inherited from his father's personality. The older he became, the more he developed Frank's features. He truly was made in his image.

Two years after Jeff was born, the Lord blessed us with another bundle of joy: a precious little girl with blue eyes and blonde hair like her brother's.

Arriving home from the hospital with the newest addition to our family, I thought about how I had always dreamed of a brown brick home in the country, a good husband, and two children with blue eyes and blond hair. I realized how God had given me my heart's desire. My cup was full and I thanked Him for His goodness.

Although Jeff was excited about having a baby sister, he didn't understand that my attention could not always be on him. One day he came to me as I was feeding Renee, and said, "I wish we would have not gotten Renee from the hospital, Mommy."

I said softly, "Why do you say that, Jeff?"

With his little head almost to the floor, he said, "Because you don't love me any more like you used to."

I tried to assure him as best I could that I loved them both the same, and that my love wasn't any less for him than it was before.

As Renee got older and Jeff discovered he had a built-in playmate, his jealousy for his sister became less and less. They became the best of friends and constant companions.

My desire to raise my children in a good religious home was always with me. When Frank's cousin asked me if Jeff could attend vacation Bible school at their church, I did not hesitate to give my approval. I thought back to when I was a child and how I loved to hear the stories in the Bible Mr. Lewis used to tell me. When Jeff would bring the projects and Bible stories home, I enjoyed studying them myself. In fact, I think I enjoyed them as much as he did.

When Renee was old enough, every summer she and Jeff went together. Seeing the children enjoying these Bible studies, I didn't think twice for my approval for them to attend Sunday school at the church. Our church didn't have anything for the young children. It was a disaster trying to keep the children still during Mass. So we would drop them off at the other church and we would go on to Mass. On our way home, we would stop and pick them up again. It was so pleasing to see their happy faces climb into the car and tell us all the things they had learned that morning. They would sing the songs about Jesus to us as we drove down the street to our home.

Unlike Jeff, Renee was always mature for her age. She seemed a couple of years older than she really was. Just as Jeff favored his father, Renee favored me. She was a very love-filled, joyous little girl. For as long as I can remember, she desired to be a mother. She kept her bedroom spotless on her own. I never had to remind her to clean it up. She loved playing with dolls, and it pleased me to see her work at being a good mother to her dolls.

One day she said to me, "When I grow up and become a real mommy, I'm going to take my baby to the hospital and get it a shot so it won't ever grow up." She continued, "I want my children to stay babies so I'll have to always take care of them and have them forever."

Frank and I had a very happy life together. We raised the children strictly but lovingly, and spent as much time with them as possible. The fruit of my chastity before marriage was surely evident: God had given me the perfect marriage I desired as a teenager.

Frank was like a kid himself, making kites and buying games for the children. Sometimes I thought he got more fun out of kite flying than Jeffery, and often joked with him about it. We were a happy family, one of the happiest I knew.

Although I was no longer part of the convent, my life was still tied to the church. I started teaching a class in Catholic-Christian doctrine at St. Joan of Arc. About twenty-five ninth-grade students attended class each Sunday morning after the early Mass. Although they had several books on doctrine to choose from, I decided to use the Bible as my textbook. I enjoyed the Bible stories and felt these ninth graders should know them too. There was one problem: the priests weren't that liberal. When the semester was half over, one of the fathers told me, "Betty, we love you, but some of the parents are complaining. They say you're teaching their children Protestantism."

It was so ridiculous I had to laugh. Protestantism? I didn't even know what it meant to be a Protestant. But the church leaders were determined and I was not renewed for the following semester. I tried to appear calm, but inside I was hurting. How could the church have done this to me? I was a natural teacher and loved children. Why wasn't I permitted to follow in my field of responsibility? We continued going to church, but my faith had been considerably weakened.

Frank had a job as a mechanic with the Pennsylvania Railroad. He was earning good pay and I was tight-fisted.

Each payday, Frank would turn over his check and tell me, "You take it, you can make money stretch farther than a Scotsman." Our bank account grew under my management. I was proud of the way I was carrying out my part of the teamwork.

Our children were our delights. My family was healthy, happy, and growing. Why did I begin to feel depressed—actually miserable at times? I decided to have a talk with God.

There was a lush green pasture behind our house. I found a pleasant spot under a shade tree and started praying out loud.

"God, what's wrong with me?" I wanted to know. "You've given me a beautiful home, a beautiful family, and good health, and yet I don't feel complete. Please tell me why I feel the way I do."

The conversation was pretty much one-sided, and when I got back to the house, things hadn't changed.

The following week, a priest who had been a member of our parish and close friend of ours, called to say he was in town and wanted to visit me. We agreed to meet for breakfast. He remarked, almost incidentally, that he had to attend a prayer meeting or he would come by that evening.

The next morning he showed up for breakfast. We were sharing coffee when I said, "Don, what kind of prayer meeting did you go to last night?"

He shrugged. "It was just something my sister asked me to attend."

"I didn't know Catholics had prayer meetings," I persisted. "Isn't that just for Protestants?"

"It's something new happening in the church," he said.

That wasn't enough for me. I wanted to know what this was all about. "Tell me more about it," I said.

"Well, actually, some things took place that were rather strange to me," he admitted. "People talk in tongues and somebody interprets it. The interpreter claims to be exercising a gift of the Holy Spirit like in the days of the disciples."

When he left, I walked with him out to his car. "Don, there's something behind my questioning," I confessed. "I'd like to find out more about these prayer meetings."

He suggested I call his sister if I had any questions. She would be more than glad to tell me all I wanted to know. I didn't waste any time making the call. Rose Ann, who lived on the other side of town, said the Catholic church was having a new, what she called Pentecostal, movement. She was all excited about it.

"We're getting to know Christ personally," she said.

"What do you mean 'personally'?" I asked.

"Look, I could talk to you all day—in fact, all week—about what we're experiencing, but the best way to learn about it is to get a book called *The Pentecostal Movement in the Catholic Church.* And get yourself a copy of the *Living Bible* and read it."

Before I hung up, she invited me to attend a meeting of the local group on the following Friday. I promised I would be there.

"Come on, Frank," I said, grabbing my purse. "We're going shopping." He seemed to catch my spirit of excitement. We drove to a Christian bookstore where I quickly found the copies. I paid for them and headed for the car.

"Is that what you got so excited about—a couple of books?" Frank asked, mildly amused.

"Don't bother me. I'm reading."

As I pored through the book about the Pentecostal movement, my enthusiasm grew. It was exciting to realize these people knew Jesus—actually *knew* Him—with such a closeness. My feeling about their personal experiences was matched only by my increasing awareness of my own spiritual emptiness. When we got home, I was completely wrapped up in the lives of these Catholic people who said they had experienced God personally.

I was too busy reading to make lunch for the children. Frank graciously agreed to handle the chore. I finished the book and reached for the New Testament, where I turned to the Gospel of John as Rose Ann had instructed. This was the first time I had ever opened a Bible without hesitation. When I got to John 3:3, the words fairly leaped out at me.

You must be born again, the Bible said. Like Nicodemus, I was confused. How could I, a person already born, be "born again"? What was its real meaning?

Trying to think of all the doctrines I had been taught, I asked, "Lord, was I born again when I had my First Holy Communion?" No, that couldn't qualify as a born-again experience. Maybe it was when I received my confirmation. The bishop slapped me on the side of the face, confirming I was a true Catholic and believed in the teachings of the Catholic church.

When *was* I born again?! I couldn't remember or know when in my life I had been born again. It bothered me so much that I turned back to that chapter again to read it over. Maybe somewhere within its pages I would be given the answer. Hours passed. It was 4:00 A.M. and I was still engrossed in God's holy Word. Frank had long since gone to sleep, grumbling about the light being on. But I couldn't stop. I had a passion to keep reading that I could not understand. I felt alive. Every nerve tingled. My heart leaped with every verse as I read all the wonderful miracles Jesus did when He was here on earth.

I don't know when I dozed off. It seemed I had barely closed my eyes when the alarm started ringing for me to get up.

I tried to encourage my husband to read the books.

"Sorry, I'm not interested," he said. "The Catholic church is just fine for me." He added meaningfully, "The way it *is*, not the way some people want it to be."

I literally couldn't wait for the next meeting of the Pentecostal group.

When Friday finally came, I asked Frank to go with me. He refused.

"You know I'm not much around groups," he said. "You go and I'll watch the kids."

Five people picked me up; one of them was Rose Ann. The meeting was to be held at a private home on the other side of town. Rose Ann warned me that the meeting would be "different."

"What do you mean, 'different'?"

She smiled and patted my hand. "You'll see."

About twenty cars were parked outside the house. I felt a bit uncomfortable as I got out of the car. My religious training was giving me doubts about the wisdom of going to the meeting. Maybe Frank was right. Maybe I didn't belong here. While I was trying to decide if I should back out, Rose Ann grabbed my arm.

In a gentle tone, she said, "Come on, Betty," seeming to feel my hesitance. "You're welcome here."

Strangers greeted me like they had known me all my life. They smiled, hugged me, greeted me with warmth. Their eyes were shining. Everywhere they were saying things like, "Praise the Lord, brother," or "Hasn't the Lord been good to you, sister?" They thought Jesus was simply wonderful.

The meeting was downstairs in the recreation room of the house. People of all ages took their chairs and a man in his late forties began playing a guitar. Everyone started singing to the music: "Jesus, I adore thee. Jesus, I love thee." It was soft, lovely, touching the heart, and the people sang it like they meant every word. I had never heard the song before, so I just listened. Song followed song, all of them unfamiliar to me. Just as I was telling myself that there really wasn't anything very different about this meeting, except that the people sang a lot, the room grew very quiet.

People were talking, but I couldn't understand what they were saying. I thought something was wrong with my hearing. Several persons raised their hands. Their eyes were closed and they made strange sounds. Although they were in the room, they weren't part of it. I realized this had to be the "speaking in tongues" Don had described. I waited for someone to interpret what they were saying.

Suddenly a woman back in the room began speaking loudly in a language I had never heard. She spoke for a long time. When she had finished, a man stood up and interpreted her message. He began with, "Thus saith the Lord." My heart leaped. The man was speaking to the people like Moses spoke to his people centuries before. When he was through interpreting, there were

31

prayer requests. The group leader opened the service to anyone who wanted to receive the baptism of the Holy Spirit. They were to go upstairs for the laying on of hands and special prayer. The meeting had ended for the general group.

I wanted to go upstairs—not because I wanted the "laying on of hands," but to see what would happen. Instead, I followed Rose Ann outside.

In the car she said, "Well, what did you think of our meeting?"

"Well. . . .," I said, with a pause. I didn't know how to finish.

"I know," she laughed. "It's different than anything you've ever seen before, right?"

"That's an understatement," I admitted.

"I want you to come back next week and learn more," said Rose Ann. "Don't give up. Keep reading your Bible and study it well. You'll soon understand what is going on."

I promised I would. When she dropped me off at my house, my head was reeling with questions.

Frank was munching on a sandwich. "How was your meeting?" he asked, sipping a glass of milk.

"Different," I said, not trusting myself to say more.

I went back for a second and third meeting. At the third gathering, they invited people who wanted to receive the baptism of the Holy Spirit to go upstairs. I wasn't quite sure I was ready for such an experience.

"Would you like to go?" asked Rose Ann. I hesitated as long as I could.

"Okay," I said, "but please go with me."

We walked up the stairs and entered the living room. We stood and watched as eight or ten people placed their hands on a young man. As they prayed, all of a sudden he began to speak in a different language. Everyone began to praise the Lord as he received the Holy Spirit.

I was next. They also placed their hands on me. They began praying that I would speak in tongues, but nothing happened.

"Don't worry, Betty," said a person who appeared to be the group leader. "Even though you haven't spoken in tongues, you've received the Holy Spirit. The gift of tongues will come later."

All that week I continued studying the Bible and praying for God to reveal himself to me.

Frank went to an early Mass the following Sunday. I went to church by myself.

I took a seat in the very last row. As the Mass began, I found myself thinking about the Bible verses I had read the preceding week.

When the priest stood up at the pulpit, I hungered for the words I had read in the Bible. I wanted to be taught about Jesus; I wanted to know how to be born again. I was so lost in my thoughts I hardly heard a word he said. As he was leaving the pulpit, I glanced at the confessional beside me. *Confess your sins to the Father. Ask Him and He will forgive you.*

My mind started to review the teachings I had been taught here. My life and heart was in the Catholic church. I believed all my life it was the only true church. What was happening to me? Why was I thinking of these things? Could what I had been taught all these years been wrong? Had I believed this unnecessarily?

I thought about the joy and peace of the people at the prayer meetings. Why couldn't these people here have the same peace and joy?

Being there had little meaning to me, and I'm sure it

showed on my face. I wanted to hear how Jesus gave His life for the forgiveness of sins, and in believing this, our joy would be full.

When I got home, I told my husband I wasn't going to go to Mass any more.

He was astonished. Angrily, he said, "What are you talking about? That's your church."

"It used to be my church," I said softly, hoping he would understand. "Frank, it just doesn't do anything for me any more; I want more of God, and I don't feel I have been taught all the truth there."

"What do you mean?" he said. "Doesn't the pope know what you are to be taught?"

"Frank, I don't know any more. God said, 'For all have sinned, and come short of the glory of God' (Romans 3:23). And that includes him," I answered.

Frank was not pacified.

"Maybe it doesn't meet your needs, but it's good enough for me," he said. "I think you're making a mistake."

That night in bed I prayed, "Lord, I want to do as you say. Please lead me to a church where I can learn more about you. I want to study the truth of your Bible." I concluded the prayer by asking for wisdom and understanding.

A few days later, while I was working in the yard, our new neighbor came up to me and introduced herself as Carol Craft. During our conversation, she asked if I attended any church. I shared with her about my Catholic faith and my experience with the prayer meetings I was attending.

"I attend Bethel Temple, a full-gospel church, so I understand this experience you've talking about," she replied.

I told her how they laid hands on me to receive what they called the baptism in the Holy Spirit. As I continued to speak about receiving this experience, she looked at me inquisitively, and said, "Betty, when did you receive Christ as your personal Savior? When were you born again?"

There it was again—"born again." As she said those words, my thoughts wandered back to the first time I read it on the day Rose Ann told me to buy a New Testament.

"You realize that the Lord said you must be born again to enter the kingdom of heaven," she said gently.

"I know," I said. "I read it in the Gospel of John. My question is, how do you become born again?"

"The Bible says, 'If thou shalt confess with thy mouth the Lord Jesus, and shalt believe in thine heart that God hath raised him from the dead, thou shalt be saved. For with the heart man believeth unto righteousness; and with the mouth confession is made unto salvation,' " she said (Romans 10:9-10).

I told her, "Maybe I haven't been born again."

She smiled wisely and said nothing.

As she let these words penetrate my mind and heart, she continued.

Tenderly, she said, "Betty, you cannot receive the Holy Spirit until you are born again. You must first become one of God's children."

Her words continued to penetrate in my mind. "Have you been born again?"

I asked her if she knew of Trinity Gospel Temple. "Two people have already mentioned this church to me, and I wondered if the Lord was leading me there," I said.

Carol said she knew of the church.

"They teach the Bible, and they are a little exhuberant at times," she said. "They clap their hands and worship openly. We're a bit more subdued at our church, but we believe the same as they do."

We embraced with a promise that we would get together and talk about the subject again.

As I walked back into the house, I thought to myself, could this church, Trinity Gospel Temple, teach me to be born again?

I called a charismatic friend I met at the prayer meeting, and she told me that Trinity was a good church.

Trinity Gospel was an interdenominational body of believers. As I looked around I was amazed to see so many familiar faces from the Catholic prayer meeting. When the minister began to ask the different denominations to stand up, I couldn't believe how many Baptists, Presbyterians, Lutherans, Catholics, Methodists, etc., were attending. The joyous songs lifted me spiritually and I felt God surely was present in this place.

As the minister spoke, it seemed he was directing every word to me. It seemed he talked about everything I ever thought or wondered about. Every word penetrated my heart. As he ended his sermon, I remember him saying, "You may be someone who may not know for sure if you are saved, born again, and you may be a regular church member. *God can care less.* He didn't start all this church business anyway. You may go to church every week. Every Sunday you do your church duty. *God can care less!* He wants you for himself!"

"What is this man saying?" I wondered. "You mean my faithfulness to the church, my obedience to attend

Mass every Sunday didn't qualify me for heaven? I'm not sure I'm saved. What should I do?"

Just as I finished the thought he said, "I want those who wish to know without a doubt that, if they were to drop dead this evening, they would immediately enter heaven to come saying, 'What must I do to be saved?'"

The rest of his words were just sounds in my ears. All I wanted to do was run and ask, "What must I do to be saved?"

Without hesitation, I ran to the altar. My friend Dorothy followed after me. I knelt down, bowed my head, and said silently, "Jesus, I want to be born again."

The minister began to pray for people who wanted to receive Christ as their Savior. I wanted him to pray for me too, but was too embarrassed to ask. Finally I told Dorothy.

She called the minister over to us and asked him to pray for me.

"Why do you want me to pray for you?" he said.

"I don't really know," I admitted. "I just want to be born again."

"Lord," he began, "you know what my sister needs. You know her heart and all of her desires. Bless her that she will know she is truly born again. Let there be no doubt in her heart. In Jesus' name I pray. Amen."

When he said "sister," the word touched me. I felt I belonged, and was part of all those other people gathered around me.

I knew I wanted to be born again, to have what these others had. I knew I wanted Jesus as my Savior. I needed God to show me what being born again really meant.

As he left me and began praying for others, Dorothy

and I hugged. No words were necessary. As I stood there, I became aware that something electrical had started in my toes and was creeping up my legs.

"Dorothy," I said, frightened, "something's happening to me. I feel like I'm going to fall."

She grew excited, saying, "Betty, that's the Lord."

The electricity swept through my body. I tried to relax. Instead I collapsed in a heap. I lay there dazed, barely aware of the others. I felt pure and clean. The vacuum I had asked God to fill months before, when I had gone into the woods near my home, had mysteriously and amazingly been filled.

I had been born again!

Being born again meant exactly what it said. I was a totally new person, a new spirit was in me. All of my other life was to be passed away, and I had a new one. God is *my* Father. It was a fantastic feeling. As the knowledge swept over me, I felt like a bubbling spring. I could barely stop myself from jumping up and praising the Lord.

Even after the meeting broke up, the tingling feeling wouldn't leave me. Driving home, I spoke to God. I asked Him what was happening to me. I was filled to overflowing with love. When I went into the house, I had to go into the bedroom to kiss my sleeping children. How sweet and precious they looked in their innocence. They stirred when my lips brushed their cheeks, but they didn't wake up. As I looked at their perfect features, given to them by our heavenly Father, my heart was overflowing.

Frank was sitting up in bed reading.

"I love you," I said, throwing my arms around him and giving him a kiss. Frank was used to my displays of affection, but this was a bit much for him. He looked at me strangely, with an amused expression, as I literally danced into the kitchen, singing praises to the Lord. He followed me.

"Betty, have you been drinking?" he began uncertainly.

I didn't answer him. Instead, I found a bottle of whiskey that had been left over from Christmas. I took off the stopper and poured it into the sink. Before Frank could move to stop me, I began doing the same thing to several bottles of beer.

"This house belongs to the Lord now," I said. "I don't want any more of this stuff in it."

"Are you crazy?" he said. Frank wasn't a heavy drinker. We used to joke about how long a bottle of beer would last around our house.

"Anything that is not of the Lord will have to go," I declared. And I gave him another kiss. He found that difficult to cope with and followed me to bed, still protesting the "useless waste" of good whiskey.

As I climbed beneath the covers, I was aware that the tingling was still present. Even though I was overjoyed at the Lord's power, I knew I had to go to sleep.

"Lord, will you please take away this feeling, just for a little while," I prayed. "I need my rest." Within minutes it was gone and I fell into a deep, untroubled sleep.

When I awoke, I felt wonderfully refreshed, as though I had a great reservoir of strength from which to draw. God was even more real to me than He had been the night before, if that was possible. The praises and joy filled my soul as I began a brand new day, a brand new life. Even my children noticed the difference.

My Bible and prayer time became a daily part of my life. It amazed me how the Lord was teaching me His Word. Sometimes the Scriptures would seem like they were popping out at me. As each day went by, anticipation grew within me for the time I would be spending in prayer and study.

Number one on my prayer list was Frank. I wanted him so much to share this new life I was experiencing. We had become two people in one house, and I wanted us to become one again.

Many times my heart was turned to the Catholic church. I prayed earnestly that they would concentrate on biblical preaching, and from its truths would become aware of some of the traditions that should not be taught, focusing on the love and saving knowledge of Jesus Christ and His soon return.

I became a regular at Trinity Gospel. As I developed friends in the church's community, I tried to share them with Frank. Always a private person, he became even more withdrawn and refused to be friendly with them. I ached inside because I wanted him to understand.

Many times I would share the different sermons I had heard at church with him. I would tell him how much joy was radiated within the services, but it had no effect on him.

"Look, Betty, I'm happy with my own church," he said. "You do what you want to do, but don't try to change me."

He turned away, red-faced, and refused to discuss it.

"You can't hide God's light under a bushel," I yelled after him.

I continued to pray for him and committed him to the Lord. I knew He knew what would touch Frank's heart. I knew one day Frank would become His child and know the blessing of God's Word.

Chapter 3

A week later, I went shopping and decided to stop at the Christian book store. I found a book entitled, *They Speak in Other Tongues*, and took it home to study. While I was reading it, an overwhelming urge to pray came over me.

"Lord, I don't know whether speaking in tongues is for today or not," I said, "but if you think it's good for me, I want it. I'm going to open my mouth. If I am supposed to have this gift, please fill my mouth with other tongues." I understand now that I was unable to receive the baptism of the Holy Spirit until I had been born again. I had the cart before the horse.

I opened my mouth and, amazingly, the Lord filled me with a new language.

I fell to the floor in shock and delight with God's strange, wonderful ways. Strange words I didn't understand nor had I ever heard bubbled out of me. I didn't know it, but Frank had come into the room. For more than twenty minutes, I was a prisoner of the Lord's Spirit, communicating in my marvelous new spiritual language. Finally I was able to look up, and I saw my husband.

"Frank, the Lord has touched me."

He didn't know whether to laugh or cry. He shook his head.

"One of us is crazy," he said, "and I don't think it's me."

He left the room, still shaking his head at my behavior.

During the next few weeks, Frank left me alone. A coolness developed between us. I couldn't decide if he was jealous over my new-found faith or concerned about the effect my "religion" was having on me. There were times when he actually tried to take my Bible away from me, insisting that I give him my attention. Other times he would retreat into his room in sullen silence, ignoring me and my friends. We invited him to study the Bible with us. He refused. He wouldn't acknowledge their warm greetings. He acted like they weren't even there. It hurt me. I wanted them to be our friends, not just my friends. I loved my husband, but we were being separated by my growing faith in a loving God.

One night Dorothy Brookins and her husband, Frank, came over for a Bible study session. My Frank, as was his custom, refused to join us.

"I'm going to work on the car," he snapped, and disappeared through the door.

We began to read the Bible and discuss the meaning of the Scriptures. Every once in a while, Frank would appear in the house to get something—a drink of water, a tool he had left. I noticed he was listening to our words, but only when he thought we weren't watching. So I did my best to ignore him. This went on for the better part of the evening.

Finally, he came in and flopped down on the living room floor. Over the past few weeks a change had come over Frank. He seemed to be getting tired earlier, without reason. It was unusual for Frank, who always seemed to have a superabundance of energy. I had made a mental note to have him see our doctor if it kept up.

Frank Brookins said, "Frank, you need Christ in your life."

My husband mumbled something and lay there, staring at the ceiling.

"I mean it," said Brookins. "Frank, I don't know why, but the Lord has impressed me to tell you a story about a friend of mine." Without waiting for Frank's approval, Brookins went on. "I worked with this guy at the mill. He and I also shared a farm together, and would often exchange farm magazines. This man was a drunkard, a mean, vicious person who had no time for his family or the Lord. I became concerned about the man's soul and told him about the Lord and his need of Him in his life. He kept telling me he didn't want to hear it. My mother was praying for him, also, and decided to give him a Bible. When the time came to exchange magazines, my mother gave him a Bible, opened and marked at John 3:16, which says, 'For God so loved the world, that he gave his only begotten Son, that whosoever believeth in him should not perish, but have everlasting life.'

"When he came into work that day he told me he had been reading the Bible for the first time in his life.

"He said he put it on his dresser beside his bed and he realized that he needed Christ in order to be saved and to be happy. Frank, I'll never forget his final words to me: 'I'm not quite ready for Him yet. But someday I'm going to come to Christ.' That was on a Thursday. On Saturday I went to work and all the men were talking. One of them asked, 'Did you hear about Joe?'

" 'No,' I said. 'What about him?'

" 'He just dropped over dead with a heart attack,' one of the men said."

Frank Brookins paused to let the words sink in.

"God was giving that man one last chance," he said very quietly. "God was calling him for the last time before he stepped into eternity. He was given that last chance through my mother giving him that Bible."

There was dead silence in the room and then he continued.

"Frank, the Lord only knows why I'm telling you this, but it's been impressed on me, and I have to obey God."

Frank grunted but never really said anything. I talked with the Brookinses a short while longer and we ended our conversation. As Frank Brookins walked out, he turned and said, "Frank, we'll be praying for you, and the Lord bless you."

Frank didn't answer him. After they left, we said little to each other. Once I tried to say something, but he cut me short.

"I'm tired," he said. "I'm going to bed."

Almost before my eyes, his health began slipping.

He would come home from work with no appetite. The dinner on the table would grow cold.

"I must have a touch of the flu," Frank would say, pushing his plate away. Night after night, he would retire to bed early, complaining that he didn't feel well. When I suggested that he see a doctor, he would

46

insist there wasn't anything really wrong with him, that he would be fine in a day or two. He tried jogging, feeling that would help him build up his endurance. It didn't seem to help. Instead, he began coughing and had trouble clearing his throat. His weight stayed the same. Frank had always been thin, but he developed a pale look, and his eyes had a sunken appearance.

I called Dr. Bronsky and made an appointment for the following day. When I told Frank about the appointment, he reluctantly agreed to go.

The nurse finally called his name and we followed her into the examination room. Dr. Bronsky, our family physician, was in his fifties and competent. He asked Frank a series of questions, including whether he had ever suffered from rheumatic fever. Frank answered no to all of them.

The doctor asked Frank to take off his shirt. He listened to his heart through a stethoscope, then took his blood pressure. His face seemed puzzled.

"Are you sure you've never had a history of rheumatic fever?" he said, still listening.

"Never," said Frank.

"Has there been any heart disease in your family?" he asked.

"My father died from heart trouble," said Frank.

The doctor put away his stethoscope and said quite casually, "Frank, I'd like to take some more tests. One of them is an EKG. You'll have to go to the hospital outpatient department."

I thought the test was unnecessary. My husband was thirty, and whoever heard of a man of thirty having a heart problem? But I kept my feelings to myself. While we were pondering the meaning behind his words, Dr. Bronsky dialed Doctors' Hospital and made an

47

immediate appointment.

The hospital was less than five minutes away. Nurses and attendants were already waiting for us when we drove up. Frank was instructed to lie down on a table, where electrodes, jelly and wires were quickly attached to him.

"This is silly," he said, attempting to smile.

The electrocardiogram took about fifteen minutes.

"Mr. Self, the doctor wants you to go home and lie down until he's had a chance to examine the results of your test," said one of the nurses.

"I've got to go to work," he protested.

"You're not going to disobey the doctor's orders," I insisted. "We're spending good money for his advice and you are going to do what he says."

Frank was just as stubborn as I was. He went over to the service station to work at his job as a part-time mechanic. I went home to fix supper, troubled with the way the day's events had turned. The phone rang.

Dr. Bronsky said, "Betty, the test results are in. I've got to ask you this question: Are you certain Frank has never had rheumatic fever?"

"He insists he hasn't," I said.

There was silence on the line before the doctor spoke. "Frank has to go to the hospital."

"When do you want him in?" I said. "He's at work."

The doctor grew angry. "My orders were for him to go home and go to bed," he said.

"Frank won't listen to anybody," I said miserably.

"Well, you call him and tell him to come home immediately," said the doctor. "As soon as he gets there, I want you to drive him to the hospital. There's something wrong with his heart."

Although I was naturally concerned, his words

didn't frighten me. I had gone through a period when my father came down with a heart problem three years earlier. He had undergone successful open-heart surgery. Even if the doctors found something wrong with Frank, I felt reasonably certain they could handle it.

Frank didn't want to leave the service station. I could sense a sort of fear, an unspoken dread of the unknown in his voice.

"Can't they leave me alone until I get through for the day?" he said.

"No, they can't," I insisted. "Now you come right home, and that means no delays." He came home, but he wasn't happy.

My husband's hospital stay lasted a week. It seemed especially long to me for what, I felt, was a minor problem. He was x-rayed and tested. Frank started coughing. He insisted it was just a cold.

When the test results were completed, Dr. Bronsky scheduled a 10:00 AM conference in Frank's room. He wasn't smiling.

"There is something seriously wrong with your heart," he said, not mincing words. "I advise you to see a heart specialist immediately." Without waiting for our reaction, he said, "Dr. Brown on our staff here at the hospital is an excellent choice. I recommend him to you."

I objected to Dr. Brown, saying I saw no reason why Frank shouldn't be examined by my father's heart specialist, Dr. Benjamin.

"That's fine," said Dr. Bronsky. "He's perfectly acceptable. I don't care who you see as long as you get yourself a heart specialist immediately."

Frank's appointment with Dr. Benjamin was confirmed for 1:00 PM that day. We carried the x-rays and examination results to him.

I had remembered Dr. Benjamin as a stocky, friendly man in a rumpled suit. He hadn't changed, and I was glad to see a familiar face. He greeted me with a warm embrace.

"What have we here?" he said, leafing through Frank's records.

The examination didn't take long. He listened intently to Frank's heart and put away his instrument.

"Frank, you're a very sick man," he said. "You have to go to the hospital right away."

Frank protested, his face turning white.

"There's nothing wrong with me," he said. "I could run up and down these halls."

"Go ahead if you want to," said Dr. Benjamin bluntly. "But we'll be carrying you to your coffin. You'd never make it. You would drop over."

My husband was afraid. He had never been in a hospital in his life. I was confident his problem, whatever it was, couldn't be serious.

"Look, my father went through this," I said reassuringly. "You'll be out of here in no time. Just cooperate with the doctors."

One thing upset Frank more than anything else.

"Doc, Christmas is just a few days away," he said, "I want to be with my family at Christmas."

Dr. Benjamin sighed. "Frank, you've got to realize one thing. You're a very sick man and you need hospitalization."

With his usual iron will, Frank insisted that he wanted to be home for Christmas, and the doctor finally relented. But he laid down a set of strict rules. There would be no walking up or down stairs. He was to remain in bed all the time he was at home. And he could walk only to use the bathroom. We both said we understood.

By the time we got home, Frank was already violating the doctor's orders. He wouldn't go to bed, and he began using the stairs. His coughing got worse. We had been home less than an hour when I phoned the doctor.

"He can't seem to stop coughing," I said.

"Take him to the hospital, no matter what he says," said Dr. Benjamin.

Frank didn't want to go. I asked him to consider me and the children, that we wanted him well.

"We need you," I said quietly. "Think of us if you won't think of yourself." That persuaded him. We got to the hospital a few minutes after 9:00 PM and the attendants whisked him into the emergency room. A giant x-ray machine was rolled up to him.

I had never seen Frank look so sick. He was exhausted from his constant, wracking coughs. He was pale, worn, and was in a cold sweat. I thought he looked at least ten years older than his age.

The doctor called me over to show me the results of the x-rays.

"Your husband's heart is at least five times the size it should be," he said, pointing out the outline of the heart. "He's in heart failure. His heart isn't pumping enough blood. We're waiting for Dr. Benjamin.

"Please don't worry, Mrs. Self," he said. "Other people have been in worse heart failure and we've saved them. We're doing all we can."

I was so frightened I felt pains in my chest and thought I was having a heart attack. Someone eased me into a chair. I was given an on-the-spot-examination.

"It's your nerves," a doctor finally said. "No heart attack."

Frank was placed in the intensive care unit on the floor for cardiac patients. I was given a shot to relax me, and insisted on seeing Frank. They took me to his room in a wheelchair.

Dr. Benjamin was busily at work, reading test results and examining Frank, who was wired to a series of strange machines.

Frank looked at me and tried to smile. He said weakly, "Don't worry, honey, I'll be all right." He looked so miserable and helpless that I had to fight to keep from crying. My visit was mercifully brief and a nurse wheeled me into the hallway. Dr. Benjamin suggested I go home and rest, pointing out that both Frank and I needed it.

"Doctor, is my husband going to be all right?" I said.

"I'm not going to lie to you," he said. "We're doing everything we can for him, but I can't even promise you he'll get out of the intensive care unit. We just don't know."

The words should have had a chilling effect on me, but I reacted just the opposite. God came into my consciousness in such a powerful way that I couldn't be frightened. His peaceful voice whispered in my ear, "Be not afraid." I knew God had control over my life and that everything would work out.

Frank's mother was a stable, level-headed woman who accepted things with a kind of, "If it must be, it must be," attitude. She drove me home. I was sleepy, almost groggy from the shot the nurse had given me. On my knees in my bedroom, I fought to stay awake while I prayed and asked God to keep my husband alive. I realized Frank didn't know the Lord. I didn't want him to spend eternity in hell. After pleading with the Lord to save him, I drifted off to sleep.

The next morning, I asked a neighbor to watch the children and phoned the church to request prayer for Frank. Brother John, the assistant pastor, came to the hospital to meet me.

His first words were, "Does Frank know the Lord?"

"No," I said. "I've been praying about it."

"Do you care if I go in and talk to him?"

"Please. I want you to," I said gratefully.

He went into the intensive care unit while I remained in the corridor. Twenty minutes passed. He finally came out the door, a huge smile on his face.

"Frank has accepted Christ," John said happily.

"Praise the Lord! Frank heeded to the nudge of the Holy Spirit, and didn't tarry his decision for Christ as did Frank Brookins's friend." I knew whatever happened, he belonged to Jesus for eternity.

I hurried into the room. Frank was smiling—not a surface smile, but from the inside. A change had indeed taken place.

"Honey, now I know why you are the way you are," he said, holding my hand tightly. "I've never felt so good, so clean inside. My sins have really been forgiven. For the first time, I believe I'm going to be all right."

My face was wet with happy tears. I kissed him, then remembered I had to get home to feed the children. As I left, Frank called, "Don't forget to bring me a Bible." A Bible! I'd bring him a dozen! That night I praised the Lord in prayer and thanksgiving.

"Thank you for letting Frank live, dear Savior," I said. "And thank you for being so real and precious to me."

Two days later was Christmas. I asked permission to allow the children to come to see their father. They honored my request, and the children and I entered his room with all his Christmas presents. A glow on his face, almost as bright as the sun, was apparent to everyone when he saw the children. I'd never seen my husband so happy.

Although the doctors weren't optimistic about Frank's chances for recovery, he began improving. In fact, his improvement was so rapid that they released him from the intensive care unit and gave him a private room on the cardiac floor. Some Christian friends from the church visited him and were amazed at how he had changed. No longer was he critical and aloof. Frank showed a warm, outgoing spirit and treated everyone who visited him with love.

A close friend said, "Your husband has truly been born again, Betty. Praise the Lord!"

One of the tests Dr. Benjamin ordered for Frank was a heart catheterization, which would permit him to view Frank's heart while it was functioning.

"These pictures will give us a better idea of what's wrong with his heart and maybe suggest some other forms of treatment," he said. Frank and I discussed the catheterization, then signed a release form. Frank was enthusiastic about the doctors taking pictures of his heart.

"Go ahead and shoot," he said, smiling. "You're not going to find anything. The Lord healed me."

But that was not to be the diagnosis.

Dr. Benjamin summoned me to his office. His face was troubled.

"Betty, we've compared these pictures with the autopsy report of Frank's father," he said. "Frank is suffering from the same disease that killed his father. There is severe damage to the heart."

He stared at the floor for a long moment.

"We give him six months to live," said the doctor quietly.

I was stunned. Fighting back my tears, I said, "How are we going to tell him? He—he has so much hope, doctor."

"We'll just have to tell him that he can't work for six months," he said.

I realized I had to be strong for both of us, as well as for the children. Above all, I didn't want to show my true feelings in front of Frank. My knees were shaky and I was sure he could detect something was wrong when I went into his room. Yet somehow I managed to smile.

Dr. Benjamin almost casually told him there had been some damage to his heart and that he would be placed on medication.

"You'll have to stay in bed for six weeks," he said, adding, "I don't see you going to work for at least six months."

Frank protested, but the doctor cut him short.

"Stop fooling yourself," he said sternly. "You're a very sick man. We're doing all we can, but we need your cooperation." That was the closest he had ever come to anger in my presence. I sensed the frustration he felt at not being able to do more.

During the next two weeks, I visited Frank daily. We set up prayer chains at the church. Everyone told me of their love for us and their concern over Frank's condition. I had decided simply to put Frank in God's hands. If he was to get better, it couldn't come from man. It had to be the work of the Lord.

I took him home from the hospital. Tired and weakened from his treatments, he went to bed without protest. He had lost considerable weight, but his changed appearance didn't bother the children. He was still "our daddy" and they didn't want to leave him alone. I cautioned them about Frank's need for rest. Secretly, I couldn't blame them for the way they felt. There was so much love between the three of them that I could hardly stand it. Sometimes I wished I had the blissful ignorance of the children instead of sharing the terrible knowledge that Frank didn't have long to live.

He started reading the Bible. One day he asked me to help him lift the mattress off our bed.

"What on earth for?" I said.

Sheepishly, Frank said, "I want to get rid of some reading material." He handed over a stack of *Playboy* magazines and other men's literature.

Shocked, I said, "You mean that I was sleeping on that!"

"Yeah," he said. "God has convicted me that I should be reading His Word—not trash like this. I'm sorry for the past, but the Lord has really changed me. I want you to know that."

We threw out the literature and Frank continued his deepening relationship with the Lord. He would spend hours in prayer. The speed he grew in the Lord amazed and delighted me. There were some days when he would spend the entire afternoon praying. And he continued his prayers even when his condition began deteriorating.

Frank's coughing spells grew worse. His breathing was increasingly labored. At night, he would gasp for air. When I couldn't stand to see him in such pain any longer, I drove him to the hospital. He was confined to a private room for two weeks. Deciding they couldn't do anything more to help him, the doctors ordered his release.

"Betty, you can do as much for Frank at home as we can here," a doctor said. "And he'll be with you and the children."

A friend told me about an evangelist in a nearby town who had a healing ministry. She suggested I take Frank there for prayer. After she described the many miracles that were taking place, I discussed it with Frank and he agreed to go. He spent the whole day in prayer.

"I'm going to be healed," he said firmly. "In fact, I'm going to eat a pizza after the service!"

Coming from him, that was incredible. Frank hadn't been able to hold anything down for days. We made up a bed in the back seat of the car and drove to the church where the services were being held. Frank was tired. We tried to get him to sit in a wheelchair, but he refused, saying, "I don't need a wheelchair. I'm getting healed tonight."

When it came time for prayer, Frank was near total exhaustion. He could barely sit up.

"What is wrong with him?" asked the evangelist. He was a short, stocky man in his forties. I told him that Frank was suffering from a rare and usually fatal heart disease. The entire congregation—there must have been three thousand people—held hands and prayed, their voices filling the cathedral. When they were finished, Frank got to his feet and slowly left the stage on his own power. I thought he was going to faint, but he somehow made it to the car. We drove home and I put Frank to bed. My friend and I went into the living room, dropped to our knees, and spent most of the night in prayer.

My heart was extremely heavy. I told God I didn't believe I could stand it if He took Frank from me.

Frank began vomiting and the pains in his stomach increased. When the pain grew especially bad, he would actually scream. Even in heart failure, he hadn't been this sick. I took him back to the hospital.

"How are you feeling, Frank?" Dr. Benjamin asked. He had just completed his examination.

"Doctor, I'm so sick," he moaned.

The doctors were perplexed over why Frank was having so much trouble with his stomach. Finally they decided that one of the medications might be causing the pain. They took him off the medicine, a heart pill, and x-rayed his stomach and chest. The pains persisted.

One day when I entered his room, the thought came to me that my husband was really going to die.

Frank was sleeping, but I felt more helpless than my husband. I tried to fight the feeling, reminding myself that as long as there is life, there is hope, but the quiet voice inside me was insistent. Frank was going to die and nothing the doctors or I did could change it. There was only one thing I could do, and that was to fall on my knees and ask God to give me peace and strength.

Several days later, Frank's condition seemed to improve. He looked and felt better and began sitting up in bed. During a routine checkup, Frank told the nurse he wanted to use the bathroom.

"Go ahead," she said. "I'll check the patient down the hall and catch you when I'm through."

Frank was in the bathroom several minutes. He came back to the bed and sat down. At the same moment the nurse came into the room. She looked at Frank and, like lightning, her expression changed. She took a second hard look.

"I'll be right back," she said. And she ran out of the room.

Almost immediately she returned and began taking his blood pressure. I looked at Frank's mother (we were the only other people in the room), not knowing what to make of her behavior. The nurse's eyes widened. She dropped the blood pressure equipment and hurried through the doorway.

Frank just sat there, seemingly unaware of what was going on. Suddenly we heard over the loudspeaker, "Code Blue. . . . Code Blue. . . ."

Nurses and doctors filled the room. They were carrying machines and equipment of all kinds. Two nurses came to us and said we would have to leave. They practically pushed us from the room.

We were out in the hall, still unaware of what was happening. Nobody would talk to us. I began a silent communication with Jesus and put everything in His hands. Moments later Dr. Benjamin and another heart specialist came down the hall. They weren't walking. As they passed us, a team of heart specialists wheeled Frank out of the room. They were heading toward the intensive care unit. Frank was moaning.

"Please tell me what's going on," I said.

Dr. Benjamin's face was pale. "I'm not sure, Betty," he said, trying to remain calm. "Frank is in deep trouble and we're trying to help him. Just stay here. When I find out what the problem is, I'll let you know. I promise."

Doors closed and we were left alone. All I could do was hug Frank's mother and whisper, "Everything will be all right. You'll see."

A nurse escorted us to the waiting room, promising to give us a report on Frank's condition as soon as she found out something.

Hours passed. Death permeated the room. Death was on my mind. What would life be like without my husband? How would the children bear it without their father? My heart cried out in silence, "Lord, why is this happening?"

The door finally opened and Dr. Benjamin slowly came out. He looked terribly weary.

"I don't think you should go in to see him now," he said.

Frantic from the waiting, determined that another door was not going to be closed in my face, I said, "I've got to see him." I began pushing past him. He held me fast.

"Betty, if you insist, I'll let you go in. But I warn you, he isn't like you've ever seen him before. It isn't pretty."

I was terrified, but I had to know. He took me by the hand and led me into the room.

Frank was stretched out on the bed. He was bent sideways, his body contorted, shaking in pain. There were so many machines, bottles and tubes attached to him that he seemed part of the machines that were keeping him alive.

"Help me," he cried. "Lord, in the name of Jesus, help me."

I couldn't do anything except cry. Tears born of fear, frustration, and a rage that had been silent too long took over me. I felt hands pushing me from the room, and I didn't resist.

"Betty, I don't want Frank to see you cry," said the

doctor. He seemed close to tears himself. "I warned you what it would be like. Now do you understand?" I nodded, too numb to speak. I was shaking uncontrollably.

"There's nothing you can do here. Go get something to eat. Do anything to occupy your mind."

"I don't want to eat. I just want to be with my husband."

Dr. Benjamin shook his head. "If you won't eat, go home and try to go to sleep," he said.

"You don't understand," I said, battling a sudden overpowering weakness. "I don't want to go home. I just want to be with Frank. Is he going to be all right?" My question was childish in the face of overwhelming circumstances, but I had to know. Or better, I had to have some sort of reassurance from this wonderful, kind, and gentle man who had grown closer to me than my own father. The crisis had brought us so close. I knew how much he loved both of us.

He took me by the shoulders and said, "I don't believe Frank will live until morning."

The final curtain had closed. The act was over. It was a time for tears, time to ask the question, "Why me, Lord?" Time for weeping and wailing and gnashing of teeth. But it didn't happen. Something else happened, something extraordinary. I realized that no longer was I looking at a dark curtain. God placed me in a peaceful scene. I was literally transported away from the hospital to another place, a valley in which the Lord himself was present. He told me I had nothing to fear. Peace reigned in my whole being.

I sensed the doctor was waiting for my response. Maybe he expected me to scream or faint, to beat my fists in rage against his chest, but I felt myself filled with a strange supernatural strength.

With a calmness that actually astonished me, I said, "What do you want me to do?"

He looked at me strangely. "Your children need you now, Betty. I want you to go home and be with them. Get all the rest you can."

"Okay," I said. I went home.

The next day was Renee's third birthday. I didn't want Frank to die on her birthday. She would remember it for years. And so I prayed, "Dear Jesus, please don't let it happen tomorrow. Lord, have mercy on a child and on me."

Dr. Sam Basil, a resident physician who was studying to be a heart specialist, met me outside the intensive care unit the following morning. When I asked to see Frank, he said he would have to check.

"That was really a rough night," he added.

"What do you mean?"

It occurred to him that I didn't know what he was talking about.

"Maybe I'm not supposed to tell you this," he said uncertainly. He shrugged. "Your husband died during the night. We had to resuscitate him."

Frank had died and been brought back to life. The Lord had heard and answered my prayers.

"Thank you, Lord Jesus," I breathed. "You are wonderful."

It was 6:30 AM when I saw Dr. Benjamin. He had been with Frank all night long and looked worn out.

He sat down beside me.

"Betty, you probably know we almost lost Frank last night. We're trying to stabilize his blood pressure. He needs a new heart. He can't live with the one he has. Maybe we can give him a new heart." He began to cry.

I could see the depth of his feelings for my husband. At that moment, I loved Dr. Benjamin more than words could express.

"If I could give him my own heart, I would," he said. Frank's blood pressure had stabilized sufficiently for me to see him. He was sitting up in bed. He looked so good I could scarcely believe my eyes. We talked briefly and I kissed him and left the room. But not before he told me, "I don't want an operation."

After a conference, the doctors told me that Frank wasn't strong enough to undergo a heart transplant. His kidneys had failed and he was suffering other complications. Even if Frank could have taken a transplant, I wasn't sure I would have approved it.

"God, you are the Great Physician," I prayed. "If there is to be a heart transplant, let it be by your hand, not by the hand of a man."

Dr. Basil, a native of India, had taken an unusual interest in my husband's case. Later, I found out why. Late one evening he came into the hospital and saw me sitting in the waiting room.

"You've been here quite late every night," he said, smiling. In his rich Indian accent, he said, "May I buy you a cup of coffee?"

"Go ahead, Betty," my mother-in-law said. "I'll stay here and call you if anything happens."

We went to the doctor's lounge and sat down. He poured the coffee.

"You are probably wondering why I asked you here," he said. "I have watched you night after night, day after day. You have spent many long hours here, knowing that your husband's chances of living are very slim. I want to know where you get your strength."

63

Without pausing, he said, "I have seen many women lose their husbands in the cardiac unit. We have had to give them tranquilizers to keep them from going into shock and to help them sleep. What keeps you from breaking down like the rest? What sustains you?"

This unusual visit was ordained by the Lord, I thought.

"Dr. Basil, there is nothing unusual about me," I began. "I have no unusual strength. All I have is Jesus. He has given me the strength that you see. Jesus gives the kind of comfort and peace of mind that no tranquilizer can duplicate."

I told him the story of Christ and the cross, and what He meant to me. He listened in silence until I was finished.

At the end he shook his head and said, "You are really quite amazing."

We finished our coffee and went back to the waiting room where my mother-in-law was sitting. He walked over to her and said, "You have an amazing daughter-in-law, Mrs. Self. Her faith in her God is beyond my understanding. Thank you for letting me have coffee with her."

Mrs. Self smiled very warmly, and said, "You're welcome."

The following day, we had lunch in the small hospital restaurant. He did his best to answer all my questions about Frank.

"Let's talk about this Jesus," he finally declared. I repeated the story of the gospel and how God had such a love for mankind that He promised never to leave or forsake us. I also told him that I believed God had the power to heal.

"As you may have guessed, I am Hindu," he said. "I

knew a man in India who could heal—at least that was what his followers claimed—but he, too, was Hindu." He was leaving that night for Toledo to attend a seminar on open-heart surgery and planned to return Sunday morning. He left, suggesting that we could meet again to continue our discussion.

When I got back to the intensive care unit, I discovered that Frank had slipped into a coma. The doctors sadly told me that it was only a matter of time before his life would end. I prayed that God would have His way in Frank's life, and that mercy and peace would come to both of us.

It was 9:30 PM Saturday night. I was so tired from my long vigils that I was half asleep in the visiting room lounge. When it came time to see Frank, I was so bushed that I told the other members of the family to go in while I rested.

I removed my shoes and was lying on the couch. It seemed I had barely closed my eyes when my mother was shaking me awake.

"Betty Ann, get up. Frank is calling you," she said. Still barefooted, I hurried to his side.

"Yes, Frank, I'm here," I said.

Very quietly, slowly, and without strength, he said, "Take my hand." One arm was attached to an assortment of tubes and bottles, so I took the hand that remained free. "Not that hand," he said, "the other one." My mother was standing on the other side, so I asked her to hold his hand. As she hung on to his other hand, Frank squeezed as hard as he could. His voice was very weak. I got as close to him as I could in order to hear his words.

"Poor guy," he said. It was barely a whisper. "That poor guy."

"What poor guy, Frank? " I said, thinking he might be dreaming or seeing something we couldn't see.

"This guy," he said, as he placed his free hand on his heaving chest, tapping it slowly. "He's gonna die." The words passed through his lips very slowly, but with assurance.

"No, you're not, Frank," I said, forcing conviction into my voice.

"Oh, yes, I am," he said, shaking his head.

My strength vanished for the moment. I gave in to the emotional upheaval at seeing my poor, helpless husband like this, and I cried bitterly. I thought of Jesus, when He was near death, how He sweat blood. I believe, at that moment, I knew how Christ had felt.

I couldn't stop myself from asking the same haunting question: "Lord, why me? Why me, who has loved you, who has prayed and believed you for a miracle. I've tried so hard to faithfully serve you. I've done everything your Word says to do. *Why!*"

There were no answers, just questions that tore at the fabric of my soul.

The nurses and the rest of the family came to rescue me when they realized my emotional state and suggested I go home and rest. They promised to keep me posted on Frank's condition, and would call me immediately if any changes occurred. No more than thirty minutes had passed when the phone rang. Even as I reached for it, I knew what the message would be.

Dr. Benjamin began uncertainly, "Betty."

"Yes."

"Betty," he repeated. And I knew.

"Betty, Frank is dead."

"I know," I said. "I knew when the phone rang."

He was a broken man, explaining that he had done

everything a physician could do, that he would have given Frank his own heart if it would have helped.

"Dr. Benjamin, nobody could have been more wonderful than you. I consider you one of the closest friends I have. Thank you for your goodness."

When I hung up the phone, the snow was falling lightly. The night was quiet and beautiful. I looked at the snow through my sliding glass door and pictured Frank as being as peaceful as the falling snowflakes.

"You won't suffer any more pain, my darling," I thought. My mood matched the serenity of the night and I knew God was working His plan in my life. Both my parents were crying.

We went to the hospital in total silence as snow fell against the windshield. I wondered how death could exist in such a lovely setting.

Everybody was at the cardiac unit: Frank's mother, his brother, whose life would be taken by this same disease a year and a half later at only twenty-three years of age, his two sisters, and other relatives. The nurses gave me the "official" news that my husband was dead. I accepted the information calmly and signed the proper papers to release his body to the funeral home.

"Would you like to go in and see him?" a nurse asked.

"No!" I said. "I want to remember him the way he was when he was alive. I saw him suffer enough."

The family argued differently. Finally I gave in to their feelings and went into his room, expecting to see him with machines and tubes still protruding from his body.

But he was lying there peacefully, as though in a deep sleep from which he would awaken. There was not a line of suffering on his tranquil face.

"Thank you, Lord, for this," I prayed, and kissed him gently on the forehead. "Goodbye, Frank."

I was up early the following morning and had breakfast waiting for Jeffery and Renee. Jeff, who was accustomed to seeing me prepare to go to the hospital, noticed something had changed.

"Mom, aren't you going to see Daddy today?" he said. He was five, a handsome boy with steady blue eyes and a lovely face. For a moment, I couldn't answer him. God, please give me the right words to say, I prayed in silence. How am I going to tell them that the man they loved so much, depended upon so much, was gone into eternity?

I took them into my arms.

"Jeff, Renee. Our daddy went home to be with Jesus."

They didn't say anything. I didn't know if they had heard me. Then Jeffery began to cry.

"You mean we'll never see our daddy again?" he said. Renee just looked at me with her big saucer eyes.

"Honey, we'll see Daddy again," I said, squeezing them with all the love I had. "We'll see him when we meet him in heaven."

Jeffery fell silent. Renee said, "Is my daddy in heaven?"

Her voice sounded so innocent and trusting that I wanted to cry. Instead, I said, "Yes, sweetheart, Daddy is in heaven."

"Will he remember me?" she wanted to know.

"Darling, your daddy could never forget you."

"Will he remember that I wanted to make him better when I played my records for him when he was so sick in bed?" she asked.

68

"Renee, whatever you did and said to your daddy, he will never forget. That I promise you."

The children walked to the window. Outside a harsh wind blew, whipping the snow in tiny hard flakes. They stared at the snow and I saw Jeffery's arm slip around Renee.

The funeral was huge. Frank had friends all over Stark County and it seemed that all of them came to see his body laid to rest. Most of the women were crying. I wasn't one of them. I knew the body inside the casket wasn't my husband, that it was just the house in which he used to live. I knew Frank was walking the streets of heaven.

Renee had gotten a birthstone ring for her birthday just a week before. When she went into the funeral parlor to view her father's body for the last time, she pulled the ring off her finger.

"I want my daddy to have my ring so he'll remember me in heaven," she said. I nodded, and she slipped it onto his little finger.

Chapter 4

When the funeral was over, we were left pretty much alone by the rest of the community. It was a new beginning for us and I didn't quite know how to handle it. Frank had been well insured, and had left us with enough money so I didn't have to look for a job. We went to work to pick up the pieces of our lives.

One person who insisted on helping us was Dr. Basil.

"Your faith is really quite remarkable," he said. "In all of my years, I have never seen anything like it."

"You'll have to come to our church and see what it's like to be a Christian," I smiled.

"That is impossible. I am Hindu."

"With God, nothing is impossible," I said.

When the children and I came down with strep throat a short time after the funeral, it was Dr. Basil who insisted on coming to our home and treating us. He refused to be paid for his services. When we had recovered, I again invited him to our church.

"Yes," he said, thoughtfully. "I believe I will come."

At the evening service, the pastor showed a film

about the rapture, *A Thief in the Night*. We went out for coffee after the service and talked about the film. I asked him what he thought about it.

"I shall be honest with you," he said. "It is very hard for me to understand. The teachings are so alien to my beliefs that I am in total confusion."

We laughed at his "total confusion" and I said, "You know, the Bible tells about the rapture. Some of us Christians believe it's coming soon."

Although Dr. Basil acknowledged the reality of Jesus and considered Him a great prophet, he said he didn't believe He was the Son of God.

It was only natural that our friendship would deepen. Frank's death had left a vacuum in my life and the lives of the children. Dr. Basil—I began calling him Sam—filled some of that vacuum. He would take the kids out for ice cream and pizza.

At one point he asked me, jokingly, if I had ever thought of becoming a doctor's wife.

"Not really," I said, laughing. "I started out to become a nun. I believe that's the last sacrifice I want to make. Besides, aren't doctors always on call?"

He smiled and accepted my humor as an answer. A great respect and feeling of admiration developed between the good doctor and myself.

One night Jeff suffered a severe asthma attack.

"Mommy, I can't breathe," he cried. It was 2:00 AM. Although I was frightened, I tried not to let it show. There was only one person I could call—Sam. He came over immediately. After examining Jeff, he gave him a shot and told me to go to bed.

"I'll stay up with him," he said.

The next morning, Jeff had a ravenous appetite. Sam had left before I got up. My mind was filled with conflicting emotions. I began wondering about this idea of being a doctor's wife. Because of my uncertain feelings, I prayed to God for guidance.

"Lord, if he is the man you have brought to replace Frank, please let me know," I prayed. "If he isn't the right person for me, please take him out of my life. I don't want to be hurt, and I don't want my children hurt."

And it happened. During the next few weeks, Sam just slipped out of my life. His work at the hospital kept him busy and I got to see very little of him. Although we remained the best of friends, the romantic attachment had cooled. The Lord had answered another prayer.

Then a different kind of crisis developed. One day Jeff came into the house and flopped onto the bed. He looked so unhappy, my heart reached out to him.

"What's wrong, honey?" I asked, sitting down next to him and brushing back his hair.

"Oh, nothing," he said in a way that told me something was very wrong.

I wanted to pursue it, but something told me it would be best to let it come out naturally. So I said casually, "Well, then, get your clothes on. We have to do some shopping."

He just lay there, in a cloud.

I put my arm around him and shook him gently.

"Hey, how about telling Mom what's bothering you," I said.

Tears began streaming down his face.

"Jeffery," I said, concerned, "please tell me what's wrong."

He said, sobbing, "Mommy, other boys' dads go to the hospital and come back home. Why didn't my daddy come back?"

He continued, sobbing into my arm as though his heart would break. "Joey's father went to the hospital and came back today. It's not fair!"

As I felt the precious warmth of his little body tremble with sobs, I prayed for guidance.

Crying harder, he said, "I don't have a daddy to fly my kite with me or to get sand for my sandbox."

"Jeffery, we don't understand why God does things the way He does. But He is God and He is master over us. I don't think He forgot you and I don't think He was being mean by taking our daddy away. He'll bring us a new daddy who will love us just as much as your real daddy did."

I gave him a squeeze, and he stopped crying. We went shopping. After I put the children to bed, I had a good talk with the Lord.

"I don't know how to ask this," I admitted. "Frank always said he didn't want his children raised without a father, the way he had been raised.

"Lord, send me a man who doesn't smoke, drink, or curse, and one who will be good to me and my children. I want a good Christian who loves you and who will serve you as I do. Amen." There! It was done, signed, sealed and delivered. Now it was up to God. I felt like I had just sent a Western Union message to the most powerful corporate head in the world. That night I slept peacefully and confidently, knowing my petition was off and flying toward its intended mark.

Some of my friends had been trying to play Cupid. They would set me up on a blind date or tell me about a certain man who seemed just "right" for me. But, somehow, none of the dates worked out. I began to feel a bit sorry for myself. After all, who wanted to be burdened with a thirty-year-old widow with two children? There were plenty of girls around who didn't have the responsibility of a ready-made family. I resigned myself to remaining single the rest of my life.

At church one day, I noticed a tall, brown-haired man in the choir. He was good looking, and possessed a bubbling sort of personality. I never saw him when he wasn't smiling. He had to be married or engaged, I felt. But I never saw him with anyone and my interest perked up. I decided to find out more about him.

When we were coming out of church, a girl friend, Helen Waznick, told me she wanted to introduce me to someone. I sighed.

"Not you too," I said. "Everybody has been trying to get me married off. Is this one short, fat, and bald, or tall, skinny, and ugly?" Helen's eyes twinkled, and we let the subject drop for the moment.

During my husband's illness, the pastor had often mentioned that Frank needed prayers, referring to him as "Brother Self." When he died, the prayers requested were for his widow and children. Some members of the church had assumed that the "Widow Self" was an older woman, as I hadn't been identified to all the congregation.

The handsome man I had noticed in the choir was Rick Gardner. I didn't know it, but he was noticing me at the same time I was noticing him. Later he would tell me, "Out of nearly one thousand people in the evening services, my eyes, for some reason, always fell on you." He said he was wondering what kind of person I was—if I was married or single. The same questions I wondered about him. God was firing arrows as fast as He could get them out of His quiver!

One night while I was in church, I asked Helen if she

wanted to come over to my house for fellowship after the service.

"Can't make it tonight," she said. "John and I have other plans, but thanks, anyway." John was her fiancé and assistant pastor of the church.

As I walked away, Rick came up to Helen and John and asked casually, "Who was that woman you just talked to?" When he discovered I was the Widow Self, he almost flipped, saying, "I thought she was an old lady." Helen grinned and asked if he wanted to meet me. Rick said he did.

The following week, without my knowledge, Helen set up a "chance" meeting for Rick and me. She pointed to him and said, "That's the guy I've been wanting you to meet." When she pointed toward Rick, I couldn't believe my eyes. Although I was shaking inside, outwardly I tried to remain calm. I wanted to meet him— I seemed drawn to him—but I was afraid. This wasn't a teenage crush. I was a widow, mother of two children, and, truthfully, I had forgotten what it was like to meet a man. Here I was, about to embark on a new male-female relationship, and I didn't know what to say or do.

"Not today, Helen," I whispered. But she wasn't taking no for an answer. Rick was standing there patiently waiting for the introduction. Helen had promised him that the two of us would meet. Even John was in on the conspiracy.

"How would you two like to go out for ice cream?" John asked, meaning Helen and me. About that time, Rick walked up.

"Hey, Rick, you can make it a foursome," John said. The snare had been set. I had been caught.

The four of us went out to Barnhill's Ice Cream

Parlor where some of the church members gathered after church. Rick was every bit a gentleman, and very easygoing, which made me more comfortable in his presence.

Two weeks later, I attended the church's Easter pageant. Rick was operating the spotlight. We went out that evening for something to eat and talked like we had known each other for years. I invited him to come to my house and help put together Easter baskets for the children. When we got home, the baby-sitter told me Jeff hadn't been feeling well. I checked him and found he had a fever. While I was playing nurse and giving him aspirins, I introduced Jeff to Rick.

"Hi," said Jeff shyly. He waited patiently until I was through doctoring him, then went to bed. Rick helped me finish the baskets.

It was getting late by that time and we all had to get up early for church the next morning. When Rick and I were through, I walked him to his car.

"See you in church tomorrow," he shouted as he drove out the driveway. I waved to him, feeling a glow that wasn't there only because of the Easter season.

The next day after service, he invited the children and me to the Brown Derby Restaurant for Easter dinner. We dined sumptuously. Jeff still wasn't feeling up to par, so we went over to my house for him to rest.

"Do you like kids?" said Renee, normally shy as a flower. When Rick assured her that he did, she climbed into his lap and laid her head on his chest. It touched me. I half expected Rick to back away, but he seemed as captivated by Renee as she was by him. It was the beginning of a love affair that would last the rest of her life.

Jeff began to feel better and started teasing Rick.

Down to the floor they went with Jeff on Rick's back. The two of them began wrestling. Renee joined in on the fun. For the first time in months, my children were laughing, giggling, and having a good time. My house was filled with warmth and happiness once again.

Rick and I began seeing each other on a fairly regular basis, but I still wasn't sure of my feelings toward him. He was divorced and had a son of his own. My marriage to Frank had been very happy and I didn't want to enter into a relationship that would hurt me or, even more, my children. I knew if I would marry, my children had to be very much a part of it too. The man I married would have to want my children to be very much a part of our lives. I wanted them to be loved and wanted as much as I was.

Rick was a new believer of six months, and I needed to be sure he had truly dedicated his life to the Lord. I wanted to be sure it was a lifetime commitment. I didn't want to walk into a relationship blindly of my own will. Only my heavenly Father in all His wisdom knows the hearts of men. I would trust Him to show me if Rick was the one He had planned for me and my children.

An evangelist came to our church for a revival meeting. He hit hard on the power of prayer. One evening he challenged the congregation to ask for three requests of the Lord, believing the Lord would answer these prayers within a week.

My prayers centered on my cousin in Pittsburgh who was on drugs and found no meaning in his life, Sam, my doctor friend, who I had witnessed to during Frank's death, and Rick.

I prayed, "Lord, if Rick is truly the one you have chosen for me, let him show something to prove how he feels, and let him tell me first before I say anything to him how I feel. If he is not the one you have chosen, please dissolve our relationship and take him out of my life."

My problem was hard to understand, unless you're a woman in love. My feelings for Rick had grown deep, while he had been treating me like a good friend. Or worse, a sister! I needed to know if his feelings had also grown.

Every night Rick and I sat in the services listening to the great wonders of almighty God. The evangelist began preaching on Wednesday night. Friday, my prayers began to be answered. That evening, my cousin from Pittsburgh called me. He said he had a sudden urge to come out to visit us. I knew the desire had been placed there by God. My Lord had answered my first prayer. John came to Canton, went to the evangelistic meeting with Rick and me, and was gloriously saved. My heart overflowed with joy.

Two nights later after Rick had dropped me off from the evening service, the phone rang just as I had gotten into bed. It was Sam, and he wanted to know what I was doing.

"What is a person usually doing at 12:30 in the morning?" I asked jokingly. "Trying to get some sleep."

He insisted on coming over to see me, even though I protested feebly that it was too late.

"Something has been bothering me," he said. "My request may sound strange to you, but I really must see you. I feel strongly there is a reason why we have been kept apart. I'm leaving Canton in the morning and I want to talk to you before I leave."

I thought about my prayer for Sam, and invited him over. By the time he arrived, the pot of coffee was perking.

Sam appeared downhearted.

"I want to know what I must do to have the same peace of mind you had when your husband died," he said. "If Jesus is real, I need Him."

"Then you have to repent of your sins and accept Him as Lord and Savior," I declared.

I shared further the need of Christ in his life, not only to receive the peace he wanted, but that it was a necessary commitment in his life.

He asked me to pray with him. We held hands, and I prayed with him to receive Christ as his personal savior. When he left my house, his eyes were filled with tears of joy and happiness. Prayer number two had been answered miraculously and gloriously.

Three days passed. I was waiting expectantly for God to answer my third prayer. My week was almost up. Wednesday evening, before I went to church, I sighed and told the Lord He must be telling me that Rick wasn't the one He had chosen for me. In obedience to Him, I decided to end my relationship with Rick after the service.

"Rick," I said, "Could you come over after the service? I'd like to talk to you about something."

"Sure," he answered, "I want to talk to you too."

What could he want? Maybe he has the same feelings about our relationship as I do. Maybe God is telling him that things are all wrong for us, I thought.

After I arrived home, I was in continuous prayer. "Lord, help me find the right words to say to Rick. Give me the courage to say what I have to. You know my feelings, and it's hard to escort this fine gentleman out of my life. But I want what you want for my life, and if Rick is not part of it, I agree," I prayed earnestly.

As Rick walked in the door, all I could say was, "Let's go for a walk down the street and back." I could always think better when I was walking, and I knew I needed all the help I could muster. It was a lovely spring night, with the smell of flowers in the air. The night seemed alive with crickets and fireflies twinkling their golden lights in the evening air. We walked along for quite a while in silence. Rick broke it, and said, "What did you want to talk about?"

A lump formed in my throat. "What did you want to talk about?" I responded quickly.

"Nope, you first," he said.

I insisted that he tell me what was on his mind before I told him what was bothering me.

"Well," he began slowly, "I guess you've been wondering about me. I realize I'm not the sort of person who shows much emotion. I've never even put my arm around you."

My heart was racing and I could barely breathe as he continued.

"I just wanted to be sure of the way I felt," he said. "I went through a real bad divorce and I didn't want to repeat it. Betty, I think I'm falling in love with you."

I thought I was going to faint.

"Because of the way I feel," he continued, not noticing my reaction, "I have to know how you feel. I don't want either of us getting hurt."

That did it. I couldn't help myself. I started jumping up and down, shouting, "Praise the Lord! Thank you, Lord!" I felt simply radiant.

Rick looked at me strangely. He had expected a reaction, but this? I guess he was wondering if I had flipped my lid.

"What did you want to tell me?" he asked.

"Rick, you were my third prayer request this last week. I too didn't want either of us getting hurt, and I want the Lord to choose my husband. The Lord has chosen you. That's why He wouldn't let me speak first tonight. My prayer was that if you were truly the one the Lord had chosen for me, then you would show me in some way how you feel," I confessed. "If you hadn't told me you loved me tonight, I was prepared to tell you I didn't want to see you any more."

He laughed and pulled me into his arms. Rick was strong, cuddly, and definitely romantic. He was sensitive and felt things deeply. Like me, he didn't want to be hurt. I gave God thanks for answering my third prayer in a week.

A week later, Rick came over to my house for coffee. I put the kids to bed and joined him in the living room, where several friends from the church had gathered.

As I kissed Renee goodnight, she said, "Mommy, could I tell Rick good night?"

"Sure, honey," I said, tucking her in.

Rick came into the bedroom and Renee hugged him.

"Can I kiss you goodnight?" she asked shyly.

"If you don't, we won't be friends any more," he said, returning the peck. She wrapped her arms around him tightly.

"Are you going to be my new daddy?" she asked, looking at him intently.

Rick was touched. "We'll see, Renee," he said.

"I'm going to ask Jesus to let you be our new daddy tonight," she answered.

Rick's heart melted, and said, "That will be fine, Renee. You sleep like an angel now, you hear, and the Lord bless you."

He joined me in the living room with a great big

smile on his face. He said, "You know what Renee just said to me?" He related to us his little talk with Renee. He added, still smiling, "I couldn't tell her no!"

That touch added something to our relationship. Three weeks later, everything seemed to fall in place. It was the merry month of May, when all living things celebrate new beginnings. We decided to get married, and set an August wedding date.

When we told the children of our plans, they acted like they couldn't believe it was happening. Almost immediately they started calling Rick "Daddy."

One of the neighborhood youngsters had been bullying Jeff and riding him about the fact that he didn't have a father. On the day we announced our plans to wed, Jeff grabbed Rick by the hand and literally pulled him outside. "Come on with me, Dad," he said.

Several kids were playing on the street. One of them was the bully. Rick didn't know what Jeff had in mind, but he was game.

"There," said Jeff, a bit defiantly. "Tell them."

"Tell them what?" asked Rick.

"What you told me," he said.

Then Rick understood. Taking Jeff by the shoulder, he told the neighborhood youngsters that he was going to be Jeff and Renee's new daddy. The effect was as though Jeff had suddenly become captain of the football team, or at least cleanup hitter in the lineup. The children stared in awe as Rick and Jeff, hand in hand, strode back into the house.

Chapter 5

We had a big church wedding. Jeff served as my ring bearer, while Greg, Rick's son, served as his ring bearer. There couldn't have been a more lovely flower girl than my own daughter, Renee.

God's presence filled the church as the wedding began. My heart fluttered with excitement and praise, knowing God surely ordained this marriage.

As I walked down the aisle, tears of happiness clouded my eyes. As I looked at the children standing there with their new adopted father and brother, I thanked the Lord for providing my family with a new beginning. I promised to serve Him all the days of my life and praised Him again and again for giving us love, comfort, and a new husband and father.

Rick was tall and handsome, almost debonair, in his cream-colored tux. I saw the love showing in his eyes, and knew what true fulfillment meant as he took me by the hand to escort me to the altar to make our vows of marriage. I realized at that point that God is truly a great God, and able to do anything.

A month after we were married, we faced our first family crisis. Rick came home from work and flopped down on the bed.

"My stomach's bothering me," he said. "Must be gas."

Flu was going around so I wasn't overly concerned. We didn't think the problem was serious enough for Rick to see a doctor. But the pain refused to go away. After three days, I told Rick he should make an appointment with the doctor.

"Naw, I'm starting to feel a little better," he said. "Why spend the money?"

I began to worry, and fear came over me like a flood. "Please, Lord, not again," I said to myself. I tried to erase the horrible thoughts I was having and began fixing dinner.

Suddenly a message formed in my mind. I was to call Rick's mother in Arizona. It was almost as though someone had spoken to me. I thought to myself, "What made me think of that?" I continued to prepare dinner, when all of a sudden, it came to my mind again. It said, "Call Rick's mother." I began to talk to myself as if I were answering the request. I said, "That's strange, why would I call Rick's mother when I know she's working at this time in Phoenix and wouldn't be home anyway?" The voice in my head persisted a third time. "Call Rick's mother."

I picked up the telephone, and as I was dialing the number, I was saying to myself, "I'll call, but no one will answer the phone." After two rings, Rick's mother answered the phone.

She said, "Hello—Hello!"

I was so astonished when she answered the telephone, I couldn't speak. Finally, I blurted, "What in the world are *you* doing home?"

"I have a bad cold and decided to take the day off," she said.

"What's with you two?"

"Oh, that explains it," I said.

"Explains what?" she answered in a puzzled tone.

I explained to her the conversation I had before I called her, and said, "The Lord must have wanted me to pray for you. He knew you weren't feeling well, and knew you were home, so He told me to call you."

Rick, hearing me talk from the bedroom, got on the extension.

"I thought you were talking to Mom," he said. "What's up, Mom?"

"Nothing serious, just a bad cold," she said. "What are you doing home?"

When Rick explained to her about the stomach trouble he was having, his mother became concerned.

"Rick, when you were a child, you had problems with your appendix," she said. "Do you remember?"

"Sure," he laughed, "but that was a long time ago."

"Maybe you should look into it," his mother said.

We hung up and I went into the bedroom.

"Do you think there might be anything to that appendix business?" I asked. It seemed impossible that that would be his problem. He didn't have any of the symptoms associated with appendicitis, like vomiting, pain in the pit of the stomach. Yet the idea wouldn't leave me. I called the doctor.

"Sounds to me like the flu," he said. "It doesn't sound serious, but if the symptoms persist, give me a call in the morning."

After dinner, I was still bothered about Rick's condition. I decided to call Dr. Benjamin for advice. He was gone, but his wife said, "There's only one real way to find out if he has appendicitis, and that's by having a blood test. I recommend you take him to the emergency room."

Rick fought against the idea of going to the hospital for a test. Yet a heavy feeling persisted in me that something was wrong, even though Rick's pain had subsided.

Finally, sitting in a chair at the dinner table, Rick said, "Something spoke to me telling me to go to the hospital."

I drove him to the hospital and he was moved into the emergency room. The old fears and memories flooded me, and I breathed a quiet prayer that the past would not be repeated.

The test came back positive. Rick had appendicitis. Surgery was needed immediately.

The surgeon told me the surgery wouldn't last over twenty minutes, but I was kept in the waiting room nearly an hour and a half. Frankly, I began to panic. I prayed for faith, and asked the Lord to put His hand on Rick.

The nurses didn't know what was going on and they were prohibited by hospital rules from telephoning into the surgical unit. They kept reassuring me that Rick was okay and the doctors would be out shortly to tell me what was going on.

Finally a doctor in a green surgical gown walked out of the operating room.

He peeled off a mask and said, "Your husband's appendix burst, and we had to perform extensive surgery to clean out the poison." He explained that peritonitis had set in and added, "Another hour and it might have been too late."

"All I want to know is if he will be all right," I said.

He refused to answer my question directly, stating only that Rick was being given antibiotics intravenously. He added that Rick had been placed in the intensive care unit.

"Come back tomorrow, Mrs. Gardner," the surgeon said wearily. "He's sleeping now."

On my way home, I was troubled by all the fears I thought I had left far behind me. I felt sorry for myself.

"Lord, why does everything have to happen to me?" I asked. I had no direct answers. I began to cry. I thought about the children. Would they become frightened of losing another father?

"Oh, Lord, please let everything be all right," I prayed. "Let no fear befall the children. Give them assurance Rick will be back home with us shortly."

When I arrived home, John and Helen were there waiting for the results of the operation. They stayed with the kids when I took Rick to the hospital. The children were in bed sleeping peacefully.

"How's Rick?" John said. "We have been praying for him." When they saw I had been crying, Helen put her arm around my shoulder.

"Betty," she said, "don't worry; Rick is going to be fine."

I returned to the hospital in the morning early. The nurse on duty refused to let me see Rick. The more I insisted, the more adamant she became. Finally I started shouting so loud that Rick later told me he could hear me in the intensive care unit.

While I was arguing with the nurse to let me see Rick, the surgeon came in to examine him.

"How do you feel?" the doctor asked him.

"Hey, Doc, I'm fine," said Rick flippantly. "Just yank this tube out of my nose and let me go home."

The doctor looked at him in astonishment.

"Go home," he repeated. "You nearly died, young man. If you would have arrived ten minutes later, you might not be here this morning. Peritonitis had set in and affected your other organs surrounding your appendix. I had to scrape all those organs."

Rick didn't protest about the tube being in his nose any more.

The nurse told the doctor about my anxiousness to see Rick, and asked if I could visit with him a few minutes. The doctor agreed to just five minutes.

Dr. Benjamin met me in the hall after I had seen Rick, and said, "Don't worry, Betty. I spoke with the surgeons and Rick is not going to die."

He must have read my mind. I tried to cling to his assurance, but I had no relief until the day the tubes came out of Rick's nose, and they began to give him antibiotics by injection instead of through the veins.

Three weeks later he returned home, much to my relief and that of the children.

God had given me many happy times during my service to Him, but the next three years were the happiest of my life. My family grew in the Lord and in love for each other. Rick and I loved the responsibilities of rearing a family.

Greg, Rick's son, became very much a part of our family too. He spent every weekend with us, and during the summer his visits were more frequent. He would sometimes spend a week at a time. I no longer had two children but three.

Renee loved her new brother. One day after Greg had spent a week with us, Renee called us to her room and gave the big announcement. She wanted to marry Greg.

"Mom," she said. "Is it all right to marry your brother? I want to marry Greg when I grow up. Is that okay?"

The thought of her loving Greg pleased me very much. I wanted so much for the three children to be compatible, and to love each other as true brothers and sister.

Rick and I smiled at each other, and I responded by saying, "We'll see, Renee, when you grow up."

Watching Jeff and Greg walk arm in arm as real brothers was very gratifying. Many times I lifted my eyes to heaven in thanksgiving, especially the time a neighborhood boy was picking on Jeff.

The boys were out playing, when one of the boys pushed Jeff. Greg came immediately to his defense. Greg knocked him down and said, "Leave my brother alone."

Our evenings were devoted to a family Bible study and prayer time after dinner. Jeff, who was nearly eight, often read out of the *Living Bible*. He loved the stories of Jesus and all the miracles He performed. He especially was drawn toward the Resurrection and being raptured from the earth. Although Renee was only five and couldn't read yet, she listened eagerly. They loved going to Sunday school and the services for children at church. Rick and I sang in the choir. It was a blessing just to be a part of the ministry of our Lord. We would seat the children in the first row of the church so we could keep an eye on them from the choir loft.

One Sunday evening as we were praising the Lord, the girl next to me nudged me to look down at my daughter. When I glanced down at her, she had her beautiful little face up toward the Lord with her hands lifted as high as she could get them, singing praises to her Lord. With joy unspeakable I thanked the Lord for such an angel he had granted me. I was so blessed to see the love she had for Him. Jeff, staying in character, had his head down praying in silence. Although his love for the Lord was just as strong, his shyness kept him from openly showing his affections.

When Brother Dave gave the announcement that he would be holding baptism for those who wanted to be baptized, Jeff was one of the first to sign up. He talked about it every day. I questioned him to be sure he knew why he was doing this.

"Jeff," I said. "Why do you want to be baptized?"

"Because Jesus commanded us to be," he said. "And besides, I want to become a part of Jesus, so I want to die with Him and be raised up a new person and share His new life, and be able to rise again after I die."

I had no question in my mind Jeff knew why he wanted to be baptized.

Jeff became a witness for the Lord. He had a friend, Joey, who was rebellious. Joey wasn't a bad boy, but he had a habit of using four-letter words when he felt like it. Although I was concerned about Joey's rather foul mouth, I didn't feel justified in telling Jeff he couldn't play with him, especially after preaching to the children to love even the unlovely. So I put the situation in the Lord's hands.

One day the boys were having lunch together at our house. Joey turned to me and said, "Mrs. Gardner, I don't say bad words any more."

"You don't?" I said. "That's wonderful, Joey."

"Jeff told me that Jesus doesn't like boys who say bad words," he declared. "He told me about Jesus dying on the cross for our sins and how we have to have Jesus in our hearts to go to heaven. He said if I expected to go to heaven, I had to be good."

Joey took a bite out of his sandwich and said, "Me and Jeff are good friends. When we go to heaven, we want to be there together."

His words touched my heart and affected me so much I rededicated my own life to God's work. I thanked Joey for his testimony and gave him a big hug.

Chapter 6

Renee entered the first grade with no problems, after an outstanding year in kindergarten. She had to take a physical examination, but passed it with flying colors.

On the first day of school, I visited a farm to buy some corn for canning. I was running late. By the time I arrived home, the children were there, eagerly awaiting the chance to report on their first exciting day at school. As I pulled into the driveway, I was aware of the lovely gold of the leaves. There was just a nip of coolness in the air, signifying that summer was being replaced by fall. Renee stood in the doorway, waving at me with a big smile.

She looked so beautiful and seemed much older than her six years. As I looked at her, I could almost picture her as a beautiful young woman, going out with young men, studying, learning the lessons of life and happiness. Yet there she was, my sweet little first grader waiting to tell me about her new adventures.

We started talking almost before I got into the house.

"We had fish for lunch," she said, pouting. "I didn't

like it. It made my stomach sick."

She wanted to help me carry the corn into the house. I told her it was too heavy, that I would take it in, but she could help me take the husks off.

Jeff was coming out of his bedroom. He had changed his clothes.

"Where were you, Mom?" he asked.

"We've got some corn to eat this winter," I said with gay abandon, showing him the stalks of fresh corn.

"Wow," he said, "can we have some for supper?"

"We sure can," I answered.

I began to prepare dinner, and Rick arrived home shortly afterwards. When he came in the driveway, Jeff dropped his bicycle and dashed to greet him, with Renee close behind.

We all sat down, asked the Lord's blessing on the food, and between mouthfuls the children were telling Rick everything that had happened that day in school. I had to smile as they tried to out-talk each other.

After dinner was over, Renee asked to go out to play. I gave her my permission and they raced out the door. I looked at Rick, smiled, and said, "Those kids are so full of life. I don't know where they get so much energy."

About an hour later, Renee came in. She was coughing.

"What's wrong, honey?" I asked.

"Nothing," she said. But she continued coughing. By bedtime, her cough was worse and she was gasping for breath.

"Maybe we should take her to the hospital," I suggested to Rick. I was worried. She had been fine at the dinner table.

"Let's just give her some cough medicine and put a

vaporizer by her bed," he said. "That will help her."

After setting up the vaporizer, we kissed her good-night. I tried to lose myself in husking the corn, but it didn't do much good. I could still hear her coughing continuously.

"There's something wrong with Renee," I said to Rick. "She's never coughed like that before. I think we should take her to the hospital, just to have her checked."

Rick agreed. I said I would stay with Jeff while he took her to get checked. I kept working with the corn, preparing it for canning.

When several hours passed and Rick hadn't returned with Renee, I began worrying. What was taking them so long? To get my mind off my daughter, I turned on the TV and tuned in the "PTL Club" program. As I was sitting there, a voice spoke to me, saying, "It's her heart."

The voice was so audible, I said, "What did you say?"

And then when I realized what I heard, fear overtook me. I got up and started trembling. I tried to talk to God, but the words came out in a shout.

"No, Lord! Oh, *no!* It can't be her heart!" I shouted. "Please, not her heart!"

I didn't know what to do. Frantically, I called my cousin, a Spirit-filled believer, and told her about Renee going to the hospital. Then I told her about the voice, and what it had said.

"Betty, you're just imagining things," she said soothingly. "Calm down. The devil is trying to scare you."

"No!" I said, weeping. "It's her heart. I know the problem is with her heart and that's what's making her cough. I know that cough. Oh, God, I know that cough."

She was silent. Then she said calmly, "Let's pray."

She began praying that the Lord would comfort me and give me a peace about Renee. Outside I heard a car door slam.

"They're back," I said. "I'll call you in a few minutes." I slammed down the receiver and ran to the door. Rick pushed open the door. I looked for Renee but couldn't see her.

"Where's Renee?" I said. "Where's Renee?"

He looked at the floor and said very quietly, "They had to keep her, Betty." He added quickly, "But she's fine. They just think that she has a touch of pneumonia."

He took me in his arms. I told him about my worries and about what I had experienced.

"You're overreacting," he said gruffly. "The doctors say it's probably pneumonia. She'll be okay."

I wanted to believe him, but I knew he was hiding something from me. I could sense it in his voice and in what he wasn't saying. Much later, Rick would tell me the truth: the doctors had discovered an enlarged heart after x-raying her, and they suspected she had the same disease my late husband had suffered. Rick had been stunned by my perception. But the doctors had insisted that he not tell me anything about their suspicions. My daughter was in heart failure.

The next morning, Renee was wide awake and glad to see me. Her coughing had settled down and she looked better than she had the night before. I stayed with her all morning. Rick came over during his lunch hour. A doctor named Harris examined Renee while we were there. Then he called both of us into the hallway.

"We suspect pneumonia, but just as a matter of routine, we'd like to have our heart specialist, Dr. Grace Hofstetler, examine her."

"If she has pneumonia, why do you need a heart specialist?" I asked suspiciously.

"I simply want to check out every possibility," the doctor said stiffly.

"Tell me the truth, Doctor," I said stubbornly. "It's her heart, isn't it?"

"No," he said. "You're overreacting." He seemed flustered.

He left abruptly, leaving the two of us. Rick had to return to work. Twenty minutes after he left, Dr. Hofstetler, a gracious and efficient woman, came into the room. Renee and I were sitting on the bed chatting.

The cardiologist introduced herself and said, "Sweetheart, could I listen to your heart?"

Renee opened her hospital nightgown to let the doctor hear the beatings of her heart. The doctor listened for quite some time.

"Renee, do you ever get pains in your chest?" she asked.

Renee shook her head.

She turned to me. "Has Renee ever had rheumatic fever?"

The words were chilling. It was the same question the doctor had asked Frank. I looked at the doctor, trying to penetrate her thoughts.

When she finished her examination, she called me into the hall.

Calmly, she said, "Renee's heart is not working correctly. She is coming out of failure, however. She's responding to the medication."

What medication? What failure?

She sensed something was wrong from the way I stared at her.

"Didn't Dr. Harris tell you?" she asked.

"They told me she had pneumonia."

"I'm sorry, Mrs. Gardner," she said. "Renee is in heart failure. We're going to do all we can for her." She said she had other children who had suffered heart failure and that they had recovered. Patting me on the arm as a reassuring gesture, she said, "Dr. Seshagiri, my associate, will be in to see Renee. I have to go to a conference and he will be taking over."

I took a deep breath. Holding back tears, I went into Renee's room and told her I had to make a telephone call and would be right back.

Rick answered the phone at work.

"Why did you lie to me?" I demanded. "And Dr. Harris—how could he have lied?"

When Rick could speak, he said, "We didn't know for sure what the trouble was. We didn't want you to get upset. The doctors thought it was either pneumonia or an infection of the heart. Dr. Harris believes it can be corrected by drugs."

Somehow his words, meant to encourage me, didn't accomplish the job. I forced them to comfort me, but I wound up drained and fearful.

During the next few days, Renee improved considerably.

Dr. Seshagiri came in to check on Renee as Dr. Hofstetler had said he would. He was an originator in the heart catheterization program at Cleveland Clinic. After his examination, he told me he wanted to go into her heart with a catheter to find out what was wrong.

"No," I said angrily, "you're not going to do that to my daughter."

The doctor had explained that she would be awake during the highly painful process, and I wasn't convinced it would do any good. He persisted.

"This is the only way we're going to know, beyond a doubt, what's wrong with her heart," he declared. When Rick supported my decision, the doctor said reluctantly that he would send her home with medication. He instructed us to watch her and said he wanted to see her in his office in a week. She was to be kept in bed for a minimum of six weeks.

For the next week, Renee slept well and acted normally. She was depressed, of course, that she wasn't in school with her friends, but she appeared to be recovering. About two weeks later, she began coughing. It grew so bad that she couldn't sleep. When I couldn't stand it any longer, Rick took her to the doctor. After examining her he assured me that she wasn't in heart failure. He said the problem might be her nerves.

"She wants to go to school so badly that it might be fouling up her nervous system," he said.

The prescriptions failed. Renee continued coughing. Friends came to me with home remedies. Ministers came to lay on hands and pray for her to be healed. I would get up during the night and literally curse the cough in the name of Jesus. Several times a night I would anoint her with oil and pray the Lord would take away this horrible coughing.

For weeks this went on. I was crying out for the Lord to help my daughter. The coughing slowed down. Finally, to our relief and in answer to our tearful prayers, the coughing stopped completely. However, a new problem developed. Renee grew very weak and had trouble breathing. Along with this she started breaking out in cold sweats. We took her to the hospital.

Several doctors conferred and gave us their finding: Renee was again in heart failure.

"We have to do a heart catheterization," one said. "There is no option. That is the only way we'll be able to find out what her problem is." This time Rick and I agreed. We had no alternative, it seemed.

They scheduled the catheterization for the following morning, and Dr. Seshagiri performed it. When he had finished, they brought her out of the operating room. Renee appeared to be sleeping soundly. Rick told me to go down to the coffee shop and get some coffee, and offered to stay with Renee in case she woke up. While I was gone, Dr. Seshagiri came to talk to Rick and me.

He told Rick, without my knowledge, that Renee had only six weeks to live.

"Your wife must not be told," he cautioned Rick. "After the way her husband died, well, she just wouldn't be able to take it."

They even gave her illness a different name for my benefit: they would call it myocarditis (which was treatable as an infection) rather than myocardiopathy, which it actually was. The doctors told me Renee was suffering from an infection of the heart that required complete bed rest for at least six weeks. She would have to remain under continuous care. Although Renee would be permitted to go home in a few days, the doctors wanted to see her at least twice a week.

Our hearts were heavy when we took Renee home. She looked so pale and helpless as Rick lifted her gently from the car to carry her into the house. She managed to smile for our benefit and to reassure us she was happy to be back in her own bed. Renee hated hospitals.

From the day she arrived home, Renee's health never improved. The disease tired her so much that she needed to be supported when she went to the bathroom.

She couldn't keep food or water down. Her symptoms were similar to what Frank had suffered in his final days on earth.

"She has the same thing Frank had," I insisted to Rick.

"No, it isn't, Betty," Rick would say, just as insistently. "You're imagining things."

A distance grew between us, despite our faith. Nothing was going to distract Rick's faith to get Renee healed. Everyone, not only Rick, was telling me, "Renee's healed, just accept it. Stop doubting."

I telephoned every healing evangelist I could think of, running up big phone bills. Every church and Christian organization I contacted promised they would pray on our behalf. Our personal lives were shattered by the experience of watching our daughter slowly slip into eternity. We held all-night prayer vigils by her bed. By faith, we tried to tell Renee that Jesus had healed her.

Renee had an answer for that which went beyond our worldly wisdom.

"Daddy, if Jesus healed me, I wouldn't be in this bed," she said wearily, but firmly. "I would be out playing with the other kids." We had no answer for that kind of logic.

Three months after Renee was stricken, my brother, Conrad, invited us to his house for Thanksgiving dinner. Thinking it would be beneficial to take Renee into another atmosphere, we wrapped her in blankets and drove over to my brother's place.

She had no appetite. She would try to eat, but that would be followed by a rush to the bathroom and violent vomiting.

"Mommy, I can't breathe," Renee cried.

We made the trip to the hospital in record time.

After x-raying her, the doctor called us aside. He appeared very nervous.

"Mrs. Gardner—Mr. Gardner," he began.

I said calmly, "Is Renee going to die?"

The doctor looked at his hands, took a deep breath.

"I wish you wouldn't have asked me that," he said quietly.

"I cannot lie to you any more, Mrs. Gardner. Your daughter is sixty percent dead. She has less than a forty percent chance of surviving."

"God can heal my daughter," I said furiously. "She will live." I didn't know it, but I had turned pale.

"Yes, I believe that too," he said. "God can make her live. He is the only one who can."

Just as I became so close to Dr. Benjamin when Frank was ill, that same closeness developed with Dr. Seshagiri.

He put his arm around me and instructed me to bring Renee into his office the following day.

"I have a new type of medicine with cortisone that may slow down the progress of the disease," he said. "Maybe it will give us more time."

After the examination the next day, the doctor shook his head and told us Renee was living on borrowed time.

"It is impossible for her to live longer than a week— two at the most," he said. "But we will try the cortisone. It is our only hope."

She was started on massive doses of cortisone in pill form that day. Almost immediately, she began swelling about the face and her stomach became bloated. One good effect of the medicine was that she began feeling better. The doctors warned us that it would be a false feeling of relief.

Her liver began deteriorating, causing her to break out in liver sores. Then, for some inexplicable reason, Renee began looking and feeling better. In fact, she felt so good that even the doctors were impressed.

After her next examination, Renee surprised Rick and the doctor by asking them if she could go to a restaurant to get something to eat.

"Why not," said Dr. Seshagiri. Overjoyed, Rick took her to a restaurant near the hospital.

During lunch, she said, "Daddy, please tell Mommy not to worry so much. I'm going to be all right. I hate to see her crying all the time. Doesn't she know I'm in Jesus' hands, and whatever happens will be okay?"

Rick assured her he would give me the message.

"What do you want for Christmas?" he said, changing the subject.

Renee gave him a complete list: a doll house and doll, games of all sorts, and a huge Christmas tree. Rick promised he and Santa would do their best.

Two days later, the doctor, impressed with her improvement, said we could let her out of bed as long as she didn't walk up and down stairs. Renee brightened, but she was still depressed because she couldn't go to school. A tutor came over daily to help her with her lessons.

Rick and I had been fasting and praying constantly for the Lord to let Renee live through Christmas. It looked like He was answering our prayers. Our hopes were that He would extend her life beyond Christmas and heal her completely.

Our church choir had a custom of singing carols to shut-ins. It was only natural that they would want to sing for Renee. We were watching TV one night when singing broke out in our front yard.

We opened the door, and Rick carried Renee to the front of the storm door to watch. When the choir was finished, we invited them inside.

Seventy people streamed into our house. Renee, who was sitting on the couch, asked them to keep on singing.

"What do you want to hear, honey?" Sister Meralene, the choir director asked. "We'll sing all night if you want."

As the songs of Christmas and hope filled our house, Rick placed his arm around me. He was looking at Renee.

"Doesn't she look like an angel," he whispered. Seeing the peace and joy in our daughter's face brought tears to our eyes. Thinking of the suffering she had been enduring, and looking at the joy on her face, I couldn't keep from crying out all that I had within me.

Christmas came. Renee started to slip.

"Aren't you going to open your presents?" I asked.

"You open them, Mommy," said Renee, restlessly. She turned to her side and looked away. I knew my daughter was very sick.

At times, she would seem to feel better. When she did, she took every opportunity to play with the toys she had received for Christmas. About a week after Christmas, she seemed to really take a turn for the worse. Her circulation was failing and her kidneys were showing signs of deteriorating. Rick and I started fasting again and praying for a miracle. I thought of the prophets of old, how they would go to the Temple three times a day to pray, and I began emulating them. My bedroom became my temple.

"Lord, everybody has told me to have faith, only believe, and everything will be all right. Lord, I don't know how to have this faith. I know you created us and gave us the very breath of life, and I know you can give Renee a new heart. But, Lord," I said in tears, "I didn't see Jesus crucified on the cross. I didn't see Him walk up to Calvary with the cross on His back. I have to believe by faith that He did this. That's all I can give you."

When I would get up from my private altar, the tears on my face represented frustration, not joy. Although my soul felt peace, I suffered pain and agony for my daughter, whose tiny body was wasting away.

Renee became frightened of the nights. This caused her to sleep all day and remain awake all night. Rick tried to stay up with her, comforting her fears with quiet talks and reassurances.

One night Renee was tossing around restlessly. Rick was lying beside her. She took him by the hand and asked simply, "Daddy, am I going to die?"

Rick told me later that a thousand thoughts flashed through his mind. His answer, from the heart, was, "No, Renee, you'll never die."

That gave her peace. Still clutching his hand, she turned over and fell into an untroubled sleep. For hours, Rick lay there, tears in his eyes, thinking and talking to God. He realized that the Holy Spirit had spoken to his heart, reminding him that none of us die, that the plan of God is for His children to pass from life to life. It was this wisdom that God had shared with Rick, allowing him to comfort a child.

When I would take her out of the tub, I wanted to cry. What my hands held tenderly was not a healthy six-and-a-half-year-old child, but a prematurely aged creature of skin and bones. My thoughts would travel back to the day she went to school. Again I saw Renee standing there, bright, beautiful, glowing with health and full of life. And now this. Nobody but the Lord knew how my heart ached.

Each time I thought I couldn't stand it any longer, God gave me strength. Only in this way could I make it from one day to the next. It was amazing, yet true: God gave me sufficient strength to accept and overcome what was happening.

As Renee's kidneys were continuing to collapse, she couldn't control her bladder any longer. Renee had always been a very particular little girl. When she realized she was too weak to go to the bathroom, that she could barely stir from the bed, it did something to her.

"Jesus, help me," she screamed. "Jesus, where are you? Mommy, Daddy, help me! Somebody please help me!"

I ran into her room, gathered her into my arms, and just held her. Our tears commingled.

"Renee, don't worry about it," I said, crying.

"Mommy, Mommy, Mommy," she screamed. "I can't stand it any longer."

At the top of my voice, I cried out, "God, where are you? Where is the mercy you talked about? Where is the miraculous healing power promised us in your Book? Where are you?! Lord, why are you letting this precious little girl who loves you so much suffer as she is? You need to help both of us!"

I just couldn't take any more.

Renee wrapped her arms around me and we held on to each other.

"Mommy, what's going to happen to me?" she cried bitterly.

I couldn't answer her. I just continued to cry out to

God to please have mercy on us.

Finally the peace came. We were exhausted, emotionally and physically, but it came over us like a blanket from heaven.

While Renee was suffering, Jeff was hurting. We would hold nightly prayer sessions for Renee.

"Jesus, please heal my sister," Jeff would pray. "She hurts so much. I want her to get better. Please take away her pains. I want to play with her again." He would always end up his prayer with a tender kiss, and would try to cheer her up.

"Don't worry, Renee," he would say, smiling. "Jesus loves you and you're going to be better very soon."

But in his own room, it was a different story.

Tearfully, he would tell me, "Mommy, I pray to Jesus to heal Renee all the time. Why doesn't He heal her?"

"Jeffery, Renee is in Jesus' hands and we must believe He knows what is best," I said. "We're believing that Jesus will make her well again."

One night Renee's heart began beating out of control. It increased in speed, simply running away with no rhythm to it. This filled her with panic, and brought a curtain of doom over me.

"I can't stand to see her suffer any more," I cried. "Either God is going to heal her or—I'll put her out of her misery myself!"

Rick said, "You're crazy. You don't know what you're saying."

But I was out of control. My eyes caught notice of the butcher knife that was on the table. I picked it up and reeled toward her room.

Rick knew what I was going to do. As I got to the dining room ready to enter the hallway to Renee's room, he tackled me like a football player. He wrestled with me on the floor and grabbed the knife out of my hand.

"Let me go!" I shouted, trying to break his hold on me. "We can't leave her like this."

"There's a reason, Betty," he said, crying. "There has to be a reason. We have to trust the Lord."

Weak and helpless, not knowing what to do or where to turn, I collapsed against his shoulder. I had no strength of my own left, no resources to draw on.

I realized I couldn't force God to do what I wanted Him to do. He was God, Master over all. If it was His will to take Renee, that would have to be what happened.

I had to release her to Jesus.

"Lord, you have brought me this far," I prayed. "You gave me a beautiful daughter for six glorious wonderful years. You know how much I love her. You love her more than I do and if you want her to join you in heaven, then take her. I know who you are, Lord of lords, and your ways are far above finding out. I don't understand why this has happened, but I accept it. I will not hold any bitterness against you. I'll serve you always."

I realized that Renee had always belonged to God. I was just the instrument that brought her into this world. My desire for her, as a parent, was for her to live on in this world. But if it wasn't God's will, I would have to accept the alternative. I thought of the Scripture when Peter rebuked Jesus because He told the disciples how He must suffer, die, and rise again the third day. Jesus said to Peter, "Get thee behind me, Satan; you are an offense to me; for you are not setting your mind on God's will, but on man's" (Matthew 16:23 paraphrased).

I was doing the same thing. I was setting my mind on man's will, my will, that Renee should live.

Rick entered the room.

"I think we're going to lose Renee," I said.

He nodded. "I know, but I could never tell you that."

"We have to accept it," I continued. "God has given me the strength to accept it. I don't know how or why, but He has given it to me."

Two days later, after I completely surrendered Renee to the Lord, she told us it was time to take her to the hospital. A peace had come over Renee also. She wanted to be with Jesus. I knew she was tired. She had fought desperately for her life these past five months, but now she was ready to surrender.

It was snowing, almost blizzard force. We bundled her warmly, and Rick carried her to the car. I held her on my lap, and we held each other for the last time, all the way to the hospital. Her warm little body against mine made an imprint that would have to last till we embraced again in that city laid with gold.

At the hospital, I registered Renee while Rick carried her to the elevator. It wasn't operating. He knew help for Renee was at the top. He had to go up three flights of stairs. Rick was running.

"Daddy, don't run," Renee admonished him, forgetting her own pain. "You'll hurt your heart."

"Don't worry about me, honey," Rick said. "I'll be all right. We have to take care of you."

As Rick raced down the hall to the room they had waiting for her, his heart was touched by the words of a little child's love. He said to himself, "She's more dead than alive, and she's worried about me. What love!" He knew what Jesus meant when He said we had to become like little children to enter the kingdom of heaven.

Within moments after she had been placed on the bed, nurses were taking her blood pressure. Dr. Seshagiri was there examining her as I entered the room. After his examination, he summoned us into the conference room.

Grim-faced, he said, "I don't think she'll live till morning."

It was almost like an instant replay of my husband's death. Fear collided with the calmness of the Holy Spirit and God won out.

With a peace and tranquility I thought I would never have, I said to the doctor, "Do what you have to do."

The doctor went a step further.

"If Renee's heart stops, I want your permission not to bring her back," he said. "If we do, she'll be in even worse pain and misery. And she'll be functioning like a vegetable. Believe me, Betty, Renee has been through hell these months; let's let her go into complete peace," he continued, with a compassion you don't see in too many doctors.

Rick and I conferred briefly and agreed with him. A kind of heavenly peace surrounded the both of us. It was the same as when Frank approached death. I knew God was holding me in His loving arms and would give me the strength and courage for what lay ahead.

Renee slipped into a semi-coma that afternoon. Although she could still talk somewhat, she didn't recognize any of us. I sat next to her as she repeatedly called my name. There was nothing I could do but pray and pray, and whisper the sweet name of Jesus.

Spending so many hours at the hospital with Renee left Jeff feeling deserted. He began asking for me to stay with him. I could feel he sensed something was terribly wrong, and he was frightened.

Rick's mother came from Phoenix to be with us. She suggested I go home to be with Jeff, and she would stay with Rick through the night with Renee.

Though it was late when I arrived home, Jeff was up waiting for me.

"I couldn't sleep, Mommy," he said. "How's Renee?"

I lay down on the bed next to my son and brought him as close to me as possible, with my arms around him.

"Jeff, Renee may go home to be with Jesus," I said, slowly.

His response sent chills all through me.

"Who's next Mom, me or you?!" he said abruptly.

I felt his pain and deep sorrow. In his short nine years he had seen half his family pass away before his eyes.

At that moment, who would ever have suspected that four months later, Jeff would have the same fatal heart disease that had taken his father, and would soon take his sister?

Jeff and I fell asleep, wrapped in each other's arms.

Up at dawn, I heard Rick and his mother come in the door. I slowly got up from bed, not wanting to disturb Jeff.

"How's Renee?" I asked.

"She seemed so well before we left, we decided to come home and get a couple of hours' rest," Rick replied. "Her blood pressure has gotten better and her breathing was almost normal. Betty, she lay there so peaceful, sleeping very comfortably," he continued. "I think she may be all right."

Two hours later, the phone rang. We had already been up getting ready to return to the hospital to be with Renee.

Rick answered the phone, and all I could hear was, "I'll be right there." Turning to me, he said, "I can't understand. Renee has turned for the worse. The hospital wants us to come right away."

I had not finished dressing, so Rick and my mother went right away, and I said I would be close behind.

As I was ready to walk out the door, the phone rang again.

"Betty," said the voice on the other end of the line. It was Dr. Seshagiri. With his voice quivering, he continued, "Renee died a few minutes ago." He paused, and then said, "I was with her when she died. She just took a deep breath and it was over. There was no struggle."

I couldn't speak. I couldn't cry. I couldn't do anything. I just stood there with the phone in my hand listening to the last chapter of my daughter's life come to an end.

I had to face Jeff with the news that Renee had died.

"God, please help me," I said prayerfully. I had no idea how to approach the subject of Renee's death. Numbly, I walked into the hallway. Jeff had been watching TV in the family room. I called for him.

"Jeff, I have something to tell you. Come here," I said.

Jeff looked at me as if he knew what I was about to tell him.

The words were out almost before I thought about them.

"Renee went to be with Jesus," I said.

I waited for him to cry, to scream, to hit me. I was prepared for anything to let him get the hurt out of his system. But he didn't do any of those things. He threw his arms around me. Then, I could feel his tears begin to run down my arms.

"Mommy, I'm going to miss Renee," he whispered. "I didn't want her to die. I'll never be able to play with her again."

"You'll play with Renee again, Jeffery," I said. "One day, we'll all be with Jesus together. There will be no more death, no more sickness, no more tears." I believed that, and I hoped Jeffery did too.

God's everlasting love surrounded us as we clung to each other, and finally words formed on my lips and I said, "Mommy and Daddy didn't want Renee to die either, Jeff. We don't understand why Jesus wanted Renee with Him instead of us, but our faith must be in His decision."

"I know, Mommy," he said, drying his tears.

He went into his room and closed the door. I did not follow him. I knew he needed to be alone.

A friend called for him to come out and play. It had been snowing most of the morning, and the air was bracing. Down the street I could see clusters of children throwing snowballs and running with their sleds. I knew Jeff had suffered enough.

"Why don't you go out and play, son," I said.

Each of us had the responsibility to go on living.

Wordlessly, Jeff turned and went outside.

I joined Rick and my mother at the hospital to help him with the funeral arrangements.

As I entered the elevator, I remembered how the snow was falling, so peacefully and lightly. It brought back memories of the day Frank had died. The same kind of snow had been falling the day he breathed his last. I could picture Renee as peaceful as the falling snowflakes. Even now Renee and her daddy were being reunited in heaven where they would share their new life forever, gloriously. I pictured them embracing and Frank lifting her over his head as he had done on earth, only now it was in the heavenly air. My heart filled with joy for the both of them.

As I left the elevator and walked to Renee's room, my thoughts returned to the body she had left behind. Along with my mother and Rick, I entered the room which was filled with the nurses who cared for her. They were all crying. I realized how dear Renee had become to the nurses. As I entered the room, they all looked up at me, moving from Renee's body, waiting for my reaction, ready to minister to me in the professional way they knew. Strength and peace welled up within me, and He stepped with me to the side of the bed where my daughter's body was lying.

"Oh, Mrs. Gardner," one of the nurses finally blurted out. "We're so sorry for you," she said, as she put her arm around my shoulders and tears filled her eyes.

My arm slipped around her waist and I said, "Thank you for your love; everything is all right."

Glancing toward Renee and the almost heavenly glow that I was sure was upon her face, I thought of Jesus' last words on the cross: "It is finished."

I whispered in my mind, "Renee, it is finished: the pain, the agony, the heartbreak you've endured these past months. Praise the almighty God of heaven. It is finished! It is finished!"

I felt tears forming in my eyes, and then trickling down my cheeks. The people in the room were ready to do what they could. But what they didn't know was that my tears were not troubled, but of joy and peace and gladness that the five months of suffering had ended.

When we returned to the house, Jeff and two of his

friends were throwing snowballs. But they weren't throwing at each other. They were tossing them underhand into the air.

"Look, Mom," said Jeff, beaming. "We're throwing snowballs to Renee. Do you think she can see us?"

"Here, Renee," one boy yelled. "Catch."

The reality of heaven had touched these children. As though in a vision, I could almost see my daughter, radiant and smiling in her new body. She was laughing as she threw the snowball back to her brother saying, "Catch, Jeff. I love you!"

Later, as I looked around the funeral home, I realized I had been in the same setting two years ago with my husband. Now it was my only daughter. As I looked at her lifeless body, God's presence was welcome as peace and strength flooded my being. Mourners began filling the room and approaching the casket. I stood there to welcome their love and receive their comfort. I knew many could not understand the peace, but I felt no remorse for my daughter. They watched and waited for me to break down. Those who shared the common bond of fellowship in Christ Jesus praised the Lord with me.

We began our new life as a family of three. Almost immediately, I noticed a change come over Rick. He grew withdrawn. He had a job as a traveling salesman, and since he was away from home frequently, Rick had plenty of time to himself. Unknown to me, he had become convinced that he had failed me and the children. His reasoning was this: as head of the household, as a believer in God, he could have done something to save Renee. Somehow he had failed us. The more he thought about it, the more depressed and uncommunicative he grew.

Rick began spending hours in prayer. He told me later, "I asked God why he let Renee die. I wanted to know if it was something I had done. The turmoil inside me was a living nightmare."

And then one day Rick got an answer.

A voice inside him spoke peacefully and calmly. The voice said simply, "Be still and know that I am Lord."

Rick realized that God was still in control of our lives, that, in fact, He had never left us.

His change in attitude was so complete that I asked him about it, and he explained what he had been going through. We both knelt and praised the Lord for answering Rick's prayer and for giving us proof that He was, indeed, still on the throne.

Jeff also suffered. His school work had been excellent. He was an A and B-plus student, but a note from his teacher informed me that his school work had slipped and his grades were failing. He just wasn't showing any interest in his work, the teacher said. I wrote back, telling about Renee's death and asking the teacher to be patient, that it would take him time to adjust.

I tried to share with Jeff about his sister, but he wouldn't respond in any way.

"I don't want to talk about her," he said angrily. "Leave me alone."

He refused to go near her room and wouldn't touch the toys they had once shared. Loneliness had set into my nine-year-old like a stone weight.

Weeks of near-total silence passed. Finally Jeff came to me. He asked a question that had been bothering him since Renee's funeral.

"Mom," he said, "if Renee went to heaven, why did

they put her in the ground?"

Explaining that a person was body, soul, and spirit, I said, "Dying is like a person leaving one house and going to another place. If we changed neighborhoods or went to another city, this house would be the same. The only difference is that we would no longer be living in it."

That didn't satisfy Jeff.

"I keep thinking about Renee being in the ground," he said. "I don't want her to be there."

"Jeff, Renee is still Renee," I said gently. "All that happened is that she changed her old house—her sick body—for a new house built for her by Jesus."

A smile slowly spread over his face.

"You mean she's in heaven and she's happy?" he asked.

"Absolutely. That's the promise God gives His children."

"That's great," he said. He hugged me and I cried, but they were tears of joy. I had my son back. God had honored another prayer request.

When Easter neared, the church leaders asked members of the congregation to try out for a Passion Play. Rick was chosen to play Pontius Pilate and Jeff played the part of a servant boy. He was excited about the play and plunged into the rehearsals with enthusiasm.

One night as we were coming home from play practice, Jeff asked, "Mom, can I get married in heaven?"

The question startled me. Fortunately Rick came to my rescue with Scripture.

"Jesus says there will be no marrying in heaven," Rick said, grinning. "If you want to do any marrying, you'll have to do it here."

Jeff said seriously, "I'm going to ask Jesus if I can

get married in heaven." He completely ignored what Rick said about no marrying in heaven. Jeff's reply stayed with me for days. I couldn't help thinking what a strange question that was for a nine-year-old child to ask.

A few weeks later, we were celebrating my sister Andrea's birthday. She had received a ceramic kit as a gift, and Jeff was making an ashtray from it. It turned out very nicely, and my mother commented how beautiful it was.

She said, "Jeff, when you get to high school you'll have to take art like your Uncle Conrad and share his talents."

Jeff continued to work on his project and said, "I'm not going to be here."

We all looked at each other in bewilderment.

"What do you mean you're not going to be here?" I asked. My heart pounded.

As he looked at me and saw the concern on my face, he perked up and said, "You don't know, Mom, the rapture may come by then."

A week later and just a month and a half after Renee's burial, he came down with pains in his stomach and started vomiting. We were all disappointed, for we had been planning a trip to Florida, on the suggestion of the doctor, hoping it would get Renee's death off Jeff's mind, and he would do better in school.

Chapter 7

"Looks like the flu," Rick said. "We'd better have him checked out."

Jeff's vomiting prompted the doctor to give him a thorough examination. This included his heart. When he was finished, he assured us that Jeff's heart was fine, his lungs were clear, and the ailment appeared to be a touch of the flu. He told us there should be no reason why we couldn't leave for Florida as scheduled.

But as the week went on, Jeff grew listless. On Sunday, the day before we were to leave, he started coughing. I didn't like the sound of it.

"Rick, could he have the same thing Renee had?" I said, scarcely daring to utter the words.

"Don't be ridiculous," Rick said. "The doctor checked his heart and said he was healthy, just five days ago. You're overreacting."

Because of my concern, he picked up a stethoscope which he had used to monitor Renee's heart and placed it on Jeff's chest.

After a few moments, he put away the stethoscope.

Casually, almost too casually, he said, "Doesn't sound like anything's wrong, but maybe we'd better take him to the doctor's office. For your sake."

Later, much later, he would tell me, "I couldn't believe what I was hearing. His heart sounded exactly the same way Renee's heart had sounded after she got sick."

Early the next morning, Rick took Jeff to the doctor. He promised we would leave on our Florida vacation as soon as they returned.

"What are you doing here?" the doctor asked Rick. "I just saw this little guy."

"He doesn't seem to be getting better," Rick said. "We thought you'd better examine him."

Jeff had been coughing almost constantly since Sunday. He looked frail and pale as the doctor told him to sit on the examining table. Jeff's back faced him. As the doctor placed his stethoscope on Jeff's chest, his eyes widened and his lips formed an involuntary oath.

"Jeff, put your shoes and shirt on," the doctor said curtly. "I have to talk to your daddy."

Rick followed the doctor into his office, with Jeff remaining in the examining room. The doctor fumbled for a cigarette lighter. His hands were shaking.

"I can't believe it," he muttered. "He's got the same damned disease as sure as I'm standing here." He paused, then continued, "We've got to get him to the hospital immediately—and hope we found it in time."

The doctor finally got his cigarette lit. He ordered Rick to give me all the details.

"Don't beat around the bush," he said furiously. "You have to tell Betty that Jeff has the same disease his sister had, and that he'll probably die. No more false hopes. We went through enough of that with Renee. And God knows I don't want her to suffer like that again."

The doctor told Jeff he had a "touch of pneumonia" that needed clearing up.

"Dad, can I still go fishing?" Jeff asked. Rick and the doctor exchanged glances.

"You might as well take him fishing," he finally said.

Rick drove to the hospital as though he was in a dream. He prayed for wisdom. I was at home visiting with my parents when the phone rang.

"Betty, I'm at the hospital," he began. He couldn't go on.

I said, "I know. It's Jeff's heart, isn't it?"

"Yes," he said. "I'm so sorry. There's nothing I can do. It's up to God."

My parents drove me to the hospital.

Dr. Harris was nearly overcome with remorse. He realized his hands and skill as a physician were handcuffed. He was facing something strange and deadly, a force so sinister that it made him tremble. An inherited heart disease was in the process of taking the second member of a family in less than four months, the third in two years.

"Jeff is going to die," he said. "I think you should tell him."

I questioned the wisdom of telling a nine-year old boy he faced imminent death.

"He has to know," the doctor said. "Children have a remarkable way of adjusting to the truth of death. They're much better at it than adults. I would tell him."

He spun around and walked away.

The heart specialist took a different course.

"Jeff has gone through much suffering," Dr. Seshagiri said. "Don't put him through the mental torture of knowing or believing he is going to die. His case isn't nearly as bad as Renee's was. This time we might have a chance to beat it."

The doctors immediately placed him on medication to remove fluids which had been filling his lungs. They also put him on digitalis to strengthen his heart. Jeff, who had been in an early stage of heart failure, was brought out of it.

And me? I became spiritually dried up.

The strain had been too much for me. There had been too many incessant prayers, too many deathbed watches, too many tears, too much fear of the unknown, too much losing people I loved, too much trying to have faith in God, too much trying to live on a day-to-day basis in the nightmarish atmosphere of hospital emergency rooms, heart specialists, and coronary units. We just couldn't take it any longer. We had run out of gas spiritually.

Rick and I looked at each other. We didn't know where to go or what to do. We were like robots.

There was only one thing to do. We really had no choice. We were Christians, living by faith, believing in God's Word. "Though He slay me, yet will I trust in Him." We turned to God.

Who else could give us hope?

The doctors couldn't help us.

God was not only the answer; He was the only answer.

I dialed the church and asked the members to put Jeff on the prayer list. We phoned all of our friends and asked them to join us in prayer on behalf of Jeff.

Van Dennis was a very close friend and a Christian. She was especially concerned about me.

"Van, I don't know if I can make it this time," I admitted. I was crying and couldn't stop.

"Dear God," she prayed, holding my hand in both of

hers. "Please have mercy on Betty and Jeff." She prayed over and over for mercy. When she was through, she asked me to come to her house.

"We'll call some of the church's staunchest prayer warriors," she promised. "Betty, we're going to assault the very wall of heaven for you and Jeff."

Jeff was too weak to make the trip to Florida. It was a tremendous disappointment to him.

Rick tried to perk up his spirits, promising that we would take him when he was stronger. Jeff didn't even have enough strength to protest. He nodded. It nearly broke my heart.

The church kept a twenty-four-hour prayer vigil going.

Jeff deteriorated rapidly. We prayed for God to spare him. We took him to a healing evangelist for prayer. His condition didn't improve.

The one bright spot in Jeff's life was mail. He loved to receive cards or letters, so I called the newspaper to put an article in the paper to ask people to send cards to cheer him up. A reporter called us and asked if he could write a story about Jeff. We agreed.

The front page article about Jeff drew hundreds of get-well cards. Children sent him tapes of them singing praises to God. A Sunday school class sent him a tape with each child wishing him well and saying they were praying for him. He received a letter from the governor of Ohio. Our congressman, Ralph Regula, a Christian, wrote to inform us he had referred Jeff's disease to the National Disease Center in Washington, D.C. Researchers were trying to discover what could be done to help Jeff, the congressman said.

Although Jeff was cheered up by the mail, physically, he continued to fail.

Rick decided to go on a fast.

"Honey, I was praying to the Lord last night and asked him what I could do to help Jeff," he said. "A voice spoke to my heart and told me to fast until I was instructed to stop. So that's what I'm going to do."

I joined him in the fast. About two weeks later, something extraordinary happened. We were in Jeff's room, talking with him, when he told us he wanted to go to sleep because he was tired. It was nearly 9:00 PM. We all prayed together. Rick and I kissed Jeff goodnight and went into the kitchen. I put a cup of tea in the microwave oven. Before the water could start boiling, Jeff called me.

"Mommy!" he called, in an irritated tone. "Mommy!"

I hurried in to see what was wrong.

"What's the matter, Jeff?" I said.

"Jesus," he said in disgust. "He keeps giving me dreams."

"What!" I said in astonishment.

"Jesus—he keeps giving me dreams," said Jeff.

"What kind of dreams?" I said.

"Oh, He's making gold in the fountain."

"Making gold in a fountain," I said puzzled. "How did you know it was gold?"

"Well, it's crystal clear like gold," he said.

I pointed to my gold wedding band and said, "Jeff, gold isn't crystal clear. It's yellow—just like my ring."

Wearily, he said, "Oh, Mom, you don't know. Leave me alone. I want to go to sleep."

He turned over and I went back to the kitchen where Rick was sitting and sipped my tea. Jeff's dream stayed in my mind.

As I lay in bed that night, I couldn't fall asleep, wondering if my son really had this dream and what it meant. I began to pray, "Lord, did Jeff really dream about you?" God answered my prayer by forming a question in my mind: What did Jeff say to you?

"Jesus keeps giving me dreams," he had said. He *keeps* giving me dreams. I thought to myself, this isn't the first time he has had a dream of the Lord.

And since I had been gone from Jeff only two minutes at the most, he couldn't have been in a deep enough sleep to be dreaming. God was revealing to me that Jeff had experienced a vision.

I thought of Acts 2:16, where Peter stood up on the day of Pentecost and quoted the prophet Joel, "And it shall come to pass in the last days, saith God, I will pour out of my Spirit upon all flesh: and your sons and your daughters shall prophesy, and your young men shall see visions, and your old men shall dream dreams."

Young men shall see visions. I knew Jeff had had a vision.

As soon as I heard Jeff stirring the next morning, I went into his bedroom to question him about his "dreams." I asked him to tell me more about the dream of Jesus he had had.

"Mom, I told you last night," he said. "Jesus was making gold in the fountain."

"How do you know it was Jesus?" I persisted.

"If you'd see Him, you'd know Him," he answered.

As he was saying it, Jeff turned toward a picture on the wall. It was a familiar artist's conception of Christ with the lamb. "And He doesn't look like that either, Mom," said Jeff firmly. "He's no hippie. He doesn't have long hair."

"What kind of hair does he have?" I said.

"Like Brother John's," said Jeff.

Brother John was the youth pastor of our church. He had his hair parted down the middle and it was to about the bottom of his ear.

Rick entered into the conversation. "What color was it?"

"Reddish brown," said Jeff, yawning. He sounded like he couldn't understand our concern. I asked if Jesus had said anything to him.

"No," said Jeff firmly. "He just stood there making gold in the fountain," he continued. "Do you remember the church play—the one I was supposed to be in with Dad, but I couldn't because I got sick? Well, you know the part when Jesus rose from the dead and He came out of the tomb with His hands outstretched. Jesus was in my dream in the same way, standing in front of a big white fountain with His hands stretched out, and real clear water was coming out of the fountain. When it touched Jesus' hands, it fell down to the ground and turned into clear gold."

I felt more confident than ever that Jeff had seen a vision. I believed my son had seen Christ as He really is. I asked him to describe what the Lord was wearing.

"He had on a long, shiny, white gown," said Jeff. "It was glowing. And the sleeves were touching His hands. He just looked at me, Mom. I didn't know what He wanted."

I asked him again, "Did He say anything to you, Jeff?"

He answered, quite disturbed, "No, I told you. He just stood there making gold in the fountain."

I tried to continue to question him, but he said to leave him alone and that he didn't want to talk about it any more.

Rick and I went into the living room, leaving Jeff to

rest. We prayed together, asking God to reveal the meaning of the vision to us. We asked the Lord to speak to us through the Bible.

Waiting upon the Lord, I thought about what Jeff had seen in the vision, the fountain, the water, and Jesus. Psalm 36:9 came into my mind. "For with thee is the fountain of life."

Jesus is the fountain of life. My heart jumped! I said to Rick, "Jesus came to Jeff and healed him. He's going to live."

Scripture began to develop in our minds. First John 3:2 came to me. "Beloved, now are we the sons of God, and it doth not yet appear what we shall be, but we know that, when he shall appear, we shall be like him; *for we shall see him as he is.*"

Jesus had appeared to Jeff in all His glory—not as man portrayed Jesus in pictures, but as He is. Jesus was going to perform a miracle in my son's life. I just knew it.

But then, the Lord gave us Colossians 3:4: "When Christ, who is our life, shall appear, then shall ye also appear with him in glory."

And I knew with a sinking heart, the miracle was not to be. The Lord was telling me, "Betty, I appeared to Jeff in my glory, and I'm going to take Jeff home with me in my glory."

Jeff was going to die! He was going to go to be with Jesus. That's what He was telling me.

I could not accept it.

"Lord, Jeff is our last child," I prayed. "I cannot conceive any more children. Please, Lord, let me raise Jeff to manhood."

The answer persisted: No. It was not to be.

I sighed, as only a mother can sigh. I had wanted to

see my son fully grown, as I had wanted his sister to grow into a lovely young woman.

I knew God's wisdom is far above our wisdom, so I did what I had to do. I surrendered my son to the Lord. But like Job, I thought it would have been better had I never been born.

Two days after Jeff told us of his vision, Jeff's friend Joey came over to spend the day. Since Jeff didn't have the strength to leave his bed, Joey sat near him, and they watched cartoons on television. I thought it would be good for someone of Jeff's age to be with him, so I left them alone. They were quietly discussing something. Later, after my son died, Joey would tell me what they had been discussing.

Jeff's vision refused to leave me. I sought to know all of its meaning. I discovered that the more I prayed, the more the Lord revealed to me.

One day as I was praying, I asked the Lord to tell me what the vision meant. If it did not mean He was going to heal Jeff, what was its meaning?

Again, the Lord started forming Scripture in my mind. It began with Isaiah 12:2-3: "See, God has come to save me! I will trust and not be afraid, for the Lord is my strength and song; he is my salvation. Oh, the joy of drinking deeply from the Fountain of Salvation" (TLB).

I had demanded a miracle; God was giving me more. He was giving me true faith in Him. We all had drunk deeply from wells of salvation.

The Scriptures continued.

Proverbs 14:27: "The fear of the Lord is a fountain of life, to depart from the snares of death."

To fear the Lord is an overflowing, ever-flowing, spring of comfort and joy; it is a fountain of life, yielding constant pleasure and satisfaction to the soul. Joys that are pure and fresh are life to the soul, and quench its thirst. It is a well of living water that is springing up to, and is the earnest of, eternal life. It is an antidote against sin and temptation, and it departs from the snares of death.

As the vision became sharply etched in my mind, I realized what Jeff had experienced. Jesus had overcome death, and so had Jeff.

The Lord's message continued with Revelation 7:17 and 21:6-7. "For the Lamb which is in the midst of the throne shall feed them, and shall lead them unto the living fountain of waters: and God shall wipe away all tears from their eyes. . . . I am Alpha and Omega, the beginning and the end. I will give unto him that is athirst of the fountain of the water of life freely. He that overcometh shall inherit all things; and I will be his God, and he shall be my son."

The Lord was showing me the condition of the place where Jeff was going, where we will all go if we drink of the fountain of life. We will be happy in the love and conduct of the Lord Jesus. He shall feed us; He shall lead us to living fountains of water; He shall put us into the possession of everything that is pleasant and refreshing to our souls, and therefore we shall hunger and thirst no more. We will be happy in being delivered from all sorrow or occasion of it. God shall wipe away all tears from our eyes. We in this world have our sorrows and shed many tears, but God himself, with His own gentle and gracious hand, will wipe those tears away, and they shall return no more. We are assured when we have overcome our present difficulties, He will give us of the fountain of life freely.

Jesus gives us His title of honor as a pledge or surety of this state of being. The greatness of this felicity is declared a free gift of God. We will be at the fountainhead of all blessedness, enjoying God and all things.

The vision began to unveil itself. The Lord was speaking to the world through a nine-year-old little boy as He did with John, two thousand years before.

Revelation 21:18 and 21. Rick and I read it together: ". . . The city was pure gold, like unto clear glass . . . and the street of the city as pure gold, as it were transparent glass."

No wonder Jeff had spoken to me like I was a child and he the teacher! Knowledge had made him mature, far beyond his years. Only God could have given my son that revelation. Jeff knew what real gold looked like—not this dull yellow thing I wore on my finger. Gold was "clear as glass." God's gold!

My son was being prepared for his coronation day.

He had seen the city he was going to live in for eternity, and he liked what he saw. How few of us are that blessed. Jeff, my dear beloved son, was blessed of God, who had given him a preview of the New Jerusalem. Could we with our limited understanding contemplate such a city as it is described? A city with streets of pure gold?

Praise my Father in heaven for His words of truth.

Revelation 22:1 shouted out, "And he shewed me a pure river of water of life, clear as crystal, proceeding out of the throne of God and the Lamb." Revelation 22:17 proclaimed, "And the Spirit and the bride say, Come. And let him that heareth say, Come. And let him that is athirst come. And whosoever will, let him take the water of life freely."

Jeff had sipped from that fountain of life. Thank you, Father.

The river of Paradise is well-watered by the fountainhead, the throne of God, and the Lamb. All our springs of grace, comfort, and glory are in God, and all our streams from Him, through the mediation of the Lamb. All the streams of earthly comfort are muddy, but the one proceeding out of the throne is clear, salutary, and refreshing, giving life, and preserving life to those who drink of it.

Revelation 3:11-12: "Behold, I come quickly: hold fast that which thou hast, that no man take this crown. Him that overcometh will I make a pillar in the temple of my God, and he shall go no more out: and I will write upon him the name of my God, and the name of the city of my God, which is new Jerusalem, which cometh down out of heaven from my God: and I will write upon him my new name."

As the reality of heaven was given to the children on the day Renee died, I had been given the true reality of heaven and life after death.

Christ is calling the Church to that duty which He promised He would enable her to do, and that is to persevere, to hold fast that which she has. Hold fast the faith, the truth, the strength of grace, that zeal, that love to the brethren. We have possessed an excellent treasure. Hold it fast, because Jesus will make a speedy appearance.

The vision filled my heart. God had spoken to my son and to me through a vision. As the Lord unveiled this vision, I saw the fountain and water representing life. Jesus is life and He flows into everyone who drinks of Him. And in Him there is no death.

The next few days passed by strangely. It was almost as if I were watching myself in a newsreel. These things were happening to me, and yet they weren't. I was part of the world; yet I was separated from it.

I can remember my friend Eleanor telling Jeff that maybe, if he was stronger next week, his parents would take him to Arizona to visit his grandparents.

Jeff answered calmly, "They'd better hurry up, because I'm not going to be here next week."

The next week, we took Jeff to see an evangelist who was holding a crusade in Detroit, Michigan. Still holding on to the belief that Jeff would be healed, in spite of all the confirmation the Lord had given me that He was going to take him home, we bundled Jeff up and made a comfortable bed in the back seat of the car and traveled to Detroit.

Jeff was placed on a cot, and we were given special seats at the front of the auditorium. After special music was provided, the evangelist stepped out on the platform, and the first thing he said, "There is someone here with a lazy left eye, and the Lord is going to heal you."

Jeff had suffered from a lazy left eye since birth. He had to wear glasses to correct it, but he never wanted them on. He just hated those glasses. During his bedtime prayers he would ask the Lord to heal that eye so he wouldn't have to wear glasses any more. When he heard the evangelist say that, he asked Rick to raise his hand since he was too weak to do it himself. He wanted his eye to be healed.

Rick held up Jeff's hand. Instantly our son's left eye became normal. A moment before it had been drooping; now it was clear and perfect.

After the service the evangelist called us to come to the back of the platform for special prayer for Jeff. After seeing my son's eye open before me, I was sure the Lord had changed His mind about taking Jeff home.

On the way home, Jeff's condition worsened. He was having trouble breathing. We prayed all the way home that the Lord would spare Jeff.

We got him into bed, and he took a short nap. After he awoke, he asked us to take him to the hospital.

"It's time," he said. "Mommy, take me to the hospital."

Rick checked his heart and blood pressure, but it had not changed.

I said, "Jeff, you're not sick enough to go to the hospital."

"Please take me to the hospital, Mom."

I didn't want to let him go. Somehow, we both knew that Jeff would never come home again.

We had gotten a puppy for Jeff and Renee a week before Renee died. After Renee died, Jeff and the puppy became very close friends.

After I finally conceded to take Jeff to the hospital, he said, "Bring me Christy, Mom, I want to say goodbye to her."

Rick brought the puppy to Jeff, and it curled up to his side.

Jeff never liked it to lick his face, but this time Jeff pulled the puppy up to his face and when it licked his face, Jeff kissed it right on the mouth, squeezed it tenderly, and handed it to me.

"Mom," he said, "take care of Christy for me. Give her extra love for me, okay?"

135

"Dad," he said, "call an ambulance. I don't want to go to the hospital like Renee did in the car."

As we carefully granted each request, we knew Jeff was prepared for the event to come.

When we arrived at the hospital with Jeff, the nurses admitted him to the children's ward. Immediately, they began ministering to him. Jeff was helpful and cheerful as the nurses tried to draw some blood. They couldn't find a vein; his veins had collapsed. Jeff found one for them, saying, "Here's one, use it," as he pointed to his arm.

The next morning, when we arrived at the hospital, the heart specialist met us in the hallway and told us Jeff wasn't in a serious state. She confidently told us imminent death was not apparent, and she would return to check on him at noon, before she left the hospital.

When she returned at noon, Jeff had already lapsed into a coma. She said she couldn't believe how fast he was failing.

All the life-saving equipment and techniques couldn't do anything. The only person who seemed to know what was happening was Jeff.

Our son was ready to go home to join his sister and father.

Rick and I didn't leave his side. We watched our beloved son as his breathing became more and more labored.

An hour before he died, Jeff opened his eyes, slowly. He couldn't speak, but he formed the word "mom" on his lips.

I bent over and brushed his hot face with my lips.

"Yes, son, Mom's here," I whispered. "Don't worry. Everything is going to be all right."

With the little strength he had left, he squeezed my

hand as if to say, "I want to go, Mom, but I want you to be okay." I gave him that reassurance, and his breathing became more relaxed.

Shortly afterwards, a nurse came in to check on him. She told us that it would be just a matter of time until Jeff's life here on earth ended. They were not able to register his blood pressure any more.

Morning had arrived, and the heart specialist returned early to see Jeff. She examined him and walked out of the room. Instantly, nurses came into the room.

"Mrs. Gardner," they said, "we're going to change Jeff's bed. You've been up all night, why don't you and your husband go downstairs for some coffee."

I sensed something was wrong. Out of fear, I snapped back at the nurse, "I'm not going anywhere. I'm staying with my son. You're not touching him, either. He's suffered enough. Just leave him alone."

They tried to reason with me. But the more they tried, the angrier I got with my protest, until I was almost shouting at them.

Suddenly, out of nowhere, this short stocky nurse appeared and put her arm around me. "Mrs. Gardner," she said, "you go downstairs and get some coffee and relax awhile. Don't worry, *Jesus* and I will take care of Jeff."

Upon hearing the name of Jesus, peace filled my soul immediately as if a tranquilizer had entered my blood stream. Rising out of my chair, I said to her, "I know, thank you."

When the nurse told us it would be a matter of time for Jeff's life to end, we called two of our closest friends to join us at the hospital. We needed all the spiritual comfort available.

Brother Carpenter, Eleanor Pasquale, Rick and I walked down the hall to the cafeteria. I know a legion of angels surrounded us as we went. No one spoke.

Rick and I had been fasting for the past three weeks. As we picked up the coffee for our meal, the Lord spoke to us at the same time.

"Eat," He said. "The fast is over."

At the same moment, Jeff, my first-born son, passed into eternity.

When we got back from the cafeteria, our minister, his wife, and several other people from the church were standing in front of Jeff's room. They tried to act as though nothing had happened.

"Jeff's dead, isn't he?" I said.

Brother Dave, our minister, said, "Yes, Betty," and we all hugged each other. Rick began crying, holding me close to him.

I wanted to see Jeff. We walked into the room. My son lay there with such an expression of peace on his face that I felt *wonderful* inside.

A song bubbled up inside of me, "One glad morning when this life is over, I'll fly away. . . ." I knew Jeff had gone to be with the Lord, and that his earthly troubles were far behind him.

The same nurse who comforted me with the name of Jesus, when they wanted me to go for coffee, came into the room and put her arm around me.

Then she said something very unusual, coming from a member of a hospital staff. She insisted on sharing with me the details of Jeff's death.

"I realize you know how terrible this disease can be," she said. "A person chokes and is in horrible pain the last moments of life. But as death approached, I held Jeff in my arms and prayed for God to take him home

138

without letting him suffer. As I prayed, the Lord filled the room with His presence. I actually felt Jeff's spirit leave his body. And I can tell you, he didn't suffer. He just fell asleep in Jesus."

My most gracious Father had sent an angel to minister to me at my son's death.

The other members of the church gathered in a circle. We held hands and began to pray, praising the Lord. We were singing joyfully. I'm sure some of the nurses thought we had lost our minds from the strain, but this was real—more real than Jeff's heart disease had ever been. We knew God was in His heaven, and that our loss was heaven's gain.

My mother came into the room, screamed, and threw herself over Jeff's body. She was filled with remorse. A nurse, who did not know me, thinking she was Jeff's mother, tried to comfort her. She then walked over to me, and said, "That poor woman. This is her third loss and the last two were her children, just four months apart."

I said, "Oh, that's not the mother; that's the grandmother."

"Oh, my, did they have to take the mother away?" she replied.

"No," I said, "I'm the mother."

She looked at me, and all she could say was, "You're the mother! You're an amazing woman. Where do you get your strength?"

"My Jesus," I explained. "He only has the power. You see, there is no fear in death for the believer. My son's spirit is in heaven at this moment and he's alive. Our hope is in the resurrection to eternal life."

God had filled my heart with such peace that I wanted—needed—to share it with others. The glorious and eternal truth of the statement that death does not end everything had to be shared. The world was filled with fear of the future and death itself. I wanted to tell the world that God removes all fear from the believer.

To the funeral director, I said, "I want a large, wide ribbon placed across the top of the casket reading, 'Son, I'll See You in the Rapture.'" I wanted it to be a token of our belief.

As I prepared for Jeff's funeral, I felt as if I was going to a wedding feast. I couldn't understand the peace and joy that was mine. Everyone who saw me was affected by it. Some were disturbed.

The day before the funeral, my mother angrily confronted me. I thought she was going to explode.

In thundering tones, she accused me of never having loved my family, that no sane person would react in the way I was reacting after having lost a husband and two children. Her words stung me. Shamed, I slipped away to my room when I arrived home and fell on my knees.

"Lord, what is wrong with me?" I prayed. "Am I abnormal, and is my mother right? Why do I feel this way?"

Like a veil of infinite softness, a presence appeared in the room. My body was immersed in it. A voice spoke to me, saying, "Betty, be not afraid. This is the peace that surpasses all man's understanding I said I would give, not as the world gives, but as I give. You are a witness of my peace."

I had heard God speak to my heart, but never like this. In the natural, I was frightened, but yet I wasn't. I can't even find the words to describe how I felt.

The presence stayed with me as I worshiped my almighty God on high. I thanked Him that through it all I could trust in Him, and asked His forgiveness for thinking He had forsaken me so many times during the preceding months, when He had been there all the time.

I arose from this sweet, sweet presence I had experienced, and as I walked out of my room, I knew anyone could think and say what they wanted. I knew my God was walking beside me in a way they could not understand.

That night I had what appeared to be a dream. I awoke as from a vision, with the knowledge that I should speak at Jeff's funeral. The Lord instructed me to use Scripture from 1 Thessalonians and 1 Corinthians. When I told Rick, he said that I should consider what I should do very carefully before going through with it.

"You've been under a lot of pressure," he said gently. "You may be imagining things."

"Why is this so heavy on my mind?" I said. "It's a feeling I can't erase. I feel God wants me to do this."

"What are you going to say?" he asked.

"I don't know," I said. "The Lord just put these Scriptures in my mind. I know He will give me the rest. He said in Matthew, 'Take no thought how or what ye shall speak: for it shall be given you in that same hour what ye shall speak. For it is not ye that speak, but the Spirit of your Father which speaketh in you' " (10:19-20).

The mortuary chapel was filled with people. Brother Dave gave me a brief introduction.

"Betty Gardner, the mother of the deceased, would like to share something with you," he said. He sat down.

When I got up to speak, I still had no idea what I was

going to say. Yet the words flowed through me as though from a source far removed from myself. The room grew very quiet.

"I know it is unusual for a mother to speak at her own son's funeral," I said. "But I would like to share what I feel about my children and husband passing on to the next world. During the time all this was happening, I thought I could never live again. But God has given me peace in my heart that passes all understanding.

"I once said I couldn't stand it if my children died from the same disease as my husband. When my husband contracted this disease, the doctor had told me of the strong possibility that the disease could be inherited by my children, especially my son, Jeff. In my own self, I lived in fear of this ever happening. And when it did strike, I thought I would begin dying too. But I want to tell you of God's sufficient grace in the hour you need it most. It's here in my entire being. Peace and comfort reign in me.

"As I stand here today, I want to comfort you, the same as you came to comfort me. I want to comfort you even more with the words of the apostle Paul.

"Before his passing, Jeff would ask me, 'What is it like in heaven? Will we be able to play ball and do the things we did down here? Is Renee doing these things now? Mom, I don't understand. You tell me Renee is alive in heaven, but why did you put her in the grave?'

"I drew him a picture of a man inside a man. Then I pointed to our home we live in, and said, 'If you go outside this house, or we move away, you're still yourself, aren't you? And what happens to this house? It still remains here, doesn't it? It's just that you don't live here any more; you've moved out. It's the same as the man inside the other man. The outer man is the house that your spirit—the real you—lives in. When you go outside your body or house, you're yourself. You've left your house behind, and it stays there.'

"Jeff responded, 'Gee, Mom, I can't wait until I go in the rapture.'

"I want to read you the words of the apostle Paul which the Lord has given me for us all. They are the verses that meant so much to my son, the verses he read all the time.

'I tell you this, my brothers; an earthly body made of flesh and blood cannot get into God's kingdom. These perishable bodies of ours are not the right kind to live forever. But I am telling you this strange and wonderful secret: we shall not all die, but we shall all be given new bodies! It will all happen in a moment, in the twinkling of an eye, when the last trumpet is blown. For there will be a trumpet blast from the sky and all the Christians who have died will suddenly become alive, with new bodies that will never, never die; and then we who are still alive shall suddenly have new bodies too. For our earthly bodies, the ones we have now that can die, must be transformed into heavenly bodies that cannot perish but will live forever. When this happens, then at last the Scripture will come true— "Death is swallowed up in victory." O death, where then is your sting?' (1 Corinthians 15:50 TLB)

"Death is a sting, isn't it? But you know, it really isn't. It is life. We can't see it. We're not on the other side. On this side it looks dark and gloomy, but on the other side there is light and happiness beyond our wildest imagination.

143

"I think of children and what a responsibility it is to raise them. We're living in a time when we need to raise our children in the Lord. We don't know when we or they will have spent our last day here on earth. What great sorrow I would have if my children were not with the Lord at this time.

'For sin—the sting that causes death—will be gone; and the law, which reveals our sins, will no longer be our judge. How we thank God for all of this! It is He who makes us victorious through Jesus Christ our Lord!'" (vv. 56-57)

Many of the mourners were openly crying. Others were smiling through tears of joy as they began to understand what I was saying. I continued to read the Scriptures the Lord had given me.

"'And now, dear brothers, I want you to know what happens to a Christian when he dies so that when it happens, you will not be full of sorrow, as those are who have no hope.' (1 Thessalonians 4:13 TLB)

"I have no sorrow because I have that hope. Those who have no hope of the resurrection are full of sorrow. They have nothing to gain.

'For since we believe that Jesus died and then came back to life again, we can also believe that when Jesus returns, God will bring back with him all the Christians who have died.' (v. 14)

"Jeff, Renee, and Frank aren't gone forever. I'm looking forward to seeing them again. And, oh, what a reunion that will be.

144

'I can tell you this directly from the Lord: that we who are still living when the Lord returns will not rise to meet him ahead of those who are in their graves. For the Lord himself will come down from heaven with a mighty shout and with a soul-stirring cry of the archangel and the great trumpet-call of God. And the believers who are dead will be the first to rise to meet the Lord. Then we who are still alive and remain on the earth will be caught up with them in the clouds to meet the Lord in the air and remain with him forever. So comfort and encourage each other with this news.' (vv. 15-18)

"So I want to comfort and encourage you with this news. We are going to be together forever when the Lord returns. There will never, never be departing again. Our lives here on earth may be extended to seventy or eighty years, but what is that compared to eternity? Even as few as six or nine years, like Jeff and Renee were granted, is nothing to an eternity without end. So I comfort you with these words, as you have comforted me these past months. Praise God! The Lord comforted me and my husband, Rick. And I know He is here to comfort you too."

I looked at them and the words flowed through me.

"I want to thank all of you for your love, especially Brother Dave and Brother John. And I have one special request to ask of you, that you love one another as Christ has loved you. None of us knows what tomorrow may bring. Love each other as though you were not going to be here tomorrow. The Bible says for us not to let the sun go down on our wrath. It isn't part of God's plan for us to know when the Lord may call someone home. So love one another, as Christ loves you. There is a great song in my heart, and it's full of love. What the world needs now is love. I ask God's blessings upon all of you."

When I sat down, Brother Dave came to the podium. His eyes glistened with tears and he looked at me with love.

"Those are the words of a true evangelist," he said. Then he led us in a brief prayer.

That day, hearts were healed and souls were saved. People who had been bitter enemies toward each other for years asked for forgiveness. Everywhere I looked there were tears of joy, repentance, and praise. And I couldn't help thinking how, out of Jeff's death, life was coming to so many. One day all of my family would be in heaven, rejoicing with so many others who had come to know Christ as their Savior. I knew the Lord had to be pleased with this harvest.

After returning from the cemetery where Jeff was buried, we returned to our house for a joyful wake. Everybody was in a happy spirit. I felt sorrow for those who couldn't understand the source of our joy. We serve a God who is triumphant, a God of hope who holds the world's future in His hands.

One of Frank's relatives was so touched by my words that he came up to Rick and said, "I don't know what you people have, but I need it. I could never have done what Betty did today."

Rick smiled, and said, "It wasn't anything she did, it was the Holy Spirit that spoke within her."

When Rick relayed the news to me, I thought, "How lovely on the mountains are the feet of them who bring good news, announcing peace, proclaiming words of happiness. Our God reigns. Yes, He reigns forever!" (See Isaiah 52:7.)

Once again, my life had a new beginning. Nothing remained of my original family. I could have no more children, but I was confident that God had a plan for my life.

I wanted those who were close to Jeff to remember him and his love for Jesus. I was going through his personal belongings and, when I came to Jeff's Bible, I thought of Joey, his closest friend. I remembered that Jeff had led him to know Jesus as his Savior and Lord, and how his life had been changed. I wanted Joey to remember the words of the Lord that Jeff had told him. I took the Bible to Joey. He received it with joy and gladness.

"Did you know Jeff knew he was going to die, Mrs. Gardner?" Joey asked me.

"Oh?" I responded.

"Remember the day I was over to visit Jeff when he was so sick? Well, he told me he was going to die and go to be with Jesus, and for me not to be afraid. He said I should always follow Jesus so we could be together again someday."

Joey was thoughtful for a moment. "Mrs. Gardner, I want to always follow Jesus so I can be with Jeff again. He was my best friend," he said. Tears began to trickle down his little face. I held him closely and tried to comfort him.

Several days later, I awoke from a dream. In the dream I had written a book. The title on the cover read, *Lord, Why Me!*

I told Rick about the dream and asked him what he thought about my writing a book. Rick thought about

147

it, and finally said, "Betty, that's between you and the Lord. If you're supposed to write this book, God will confirm your dream."

I don't doubt anything any more.

After Rick went to work, I began cleaning up the house. A neighbor, a close Christian friend, came over to see me. As we talked over a cup of tea, she said, "Betty, this may sound strange, but I believe the Lord wants you to write a book."

I almost knocked my cup over in my excitement. "Why do you say that?" I asked, trying to remain calm.

"Well, the Lord put it in my heart this morning, and I couldn't stop thinking about it, so I had to come over and talk to you about it. To top it all, the title, *Lord, Why Me!* keeps coming to my mind."

I could hardly believe my ears. Rick had said that the Lord would confirm it if it was to be. I shared with her the dream I'd had and what Rick had said.

"I believe the Lord wants you to write a book, Betty," she said.

Here it is, Lord.

Chapter 8

Rick and I were alone now. As Christy, our miniature schnauzer, wriggled on our laps for attention, we remembered Jeff's last request: "Take care of Christy."

As Rick and I reflected over the many events which had taken place in just the past nine months, we came to realize the omnipotence and omniscience of our God. We talked about the abundant mercies of God and how He walked with us through the valley of death, and the truth of God's words when He said he would never leave us nor forsake us.

We understood that we had been led through these crises through the sovereign will of God so that we may be brought to the place of being able to say, "I know Him." Not just know Him intellectually, but to experience Him and know Him. These experiences were not allowed into our lives to break us, but rather to make us. They did not come to destroy us, but rather to disciple us in Christ. If we've never been on stormy seas, how can we ever know that Jesus can calm those seas?

If we've never been down in the dunghills of life, how will we know He's able to raise us up? God didn't lose the reins for a little while. He brought us through that we may know and understand a maturity that is in Christ. That we may know Him and the power of His resurrected presence.

We thought about Greg, and we truly understood God's wisdom in taking him out of our lives to be with his mother and stepfather. Judging from Greg's reaction to Jeff's and Renee's deaths when first informed about it, we knew what the reaction would be had he been there to witness the suffering of a brother and sister he dearly loved.

Our life as parents had ended and we understood. It was now time to look ahead, to pursue the paths our lives would wend.

About a week later, the Lord impressed upon me that Rick and I should go to Bible school. We began to pray, asking the Lord where He wanted us to go. An elder from our church told me that a Bible school, Christ for the Nations, in Dallas, would be a choice to consider. We sent for information and it seemed to fit every need we were looking for. So we rented our home in Ohio and enrolled. After studying for two years, including summer school, we would receive our degree in theology.

There were many great testimonies given by special guest speakers at school. God replaced eyeballs, gave new kidneys, cancers were healed, and many more miracles were reported. I began to wonder what I was doing there. What was I training to be a minister for? What was I going to share about God? That my God was so great, He took my whole family? He never answered any of my prayers for healing. I soon forgot the peace the Lord had so miraculously given me. The devil was doing his accusing and hassling. My attitude became so negative, I wanted to leave college.

"I believe we've missed God's calling, Rick," I said. "This was not God's will for us to come here. I want to leave."

"Honey," he said, "be patient. Maybe we'll learn where we failed, if nothing else. Let's at least finish this year's semester."

I knew how much Rick was enjoying school, and for his sake I agreed to stay.

Dr. Monroe, our school chancellor, put together a trip to Israel as part of our student ministry. The "Missionary Learning Journey" was designed to help us understand how to better minister to the Jewish people and to see the land where our Lord Jesus walked.

Rick and I had always desired to go to Israel, so we signed up for the journey.

While at Haifa University, we met with a group of Israeli students to share our studies at our college, and for them to share their studies with us. We talked about our love for Israel and our belief in the Messiah. The assistant dean was so impressed, he invited us to his home that evening to share with other Israelis about our beliefs. He said one of the great professors of religion in Israel would be there.

Our group was in prayer the remainder of the day. We knew the Lord had opened the door to share the love of Christ with these Israelis.

We arrived at his home with a warm welcome, accompanied with a table full of food. The room was full of people. There were about fifteen Israelis, besides our group. We all sat down and ate. Then we began to share. We started talking about the Arab-Israeli conflict. We were spending quite some time talking about it. Suddenly, the professor of religion blurted out, "We're not here to talk about politics. We want to know about your religious beliefs, and your affectionate interest in Israel."

Dr. Monroe, in response, said, "We're Biblical Zionists. We believe Israel is preordained to be here as a nation as prophesied by the prophets." He further stated that we believed the Messiah is Jesus Christ and that He is coming again to set up His throne in Jerusalem. He closed graciously by asking the Israelis how they felt about the Messiah.

An elderly woman said she believed the Messiah was a form of inner peace. She described watching her family die in a German concentration camp during World War II. As a child she said she had read of how fine the grapes of Israel were, how big and juicy. After the war, she was exiled to Israel to work on a kibbutz. There for the first time in her life, she tasted the grapes and wine of Israel.

"Instantly I felt inner peace," she said, smiling. "It was as though my life had suddenly been fulfilled."

When she finished, the professor sitting next to me described the Messiah as a political peace. I was sitting there, listening, totally unaware of what was to come next.

Suddenly a thought filled my head.

"Tell them of Jeff's vision," the voice said. "Tell them why you believe Jesus is the Messiah and why you believe the Messiah is a person."

We had been warned by Dr. Monroe not to speak about Christ, that it was better for us to show love rather than to push Christianity on the people.

I sat back in my chair, and I thought to myself, "What made me think of telling Jeff's vision?" I dismissed the thought and continued to listen to the conversation. Again it happened.

"Tell them why you believe Jesus is the Messiah and why you believe He is a person."

"Devil, I rebuke you," I said.

The thought could only have come from him. He would love to see the whole evening ruined.

Again the thought returned. But with more emphasis this time.

"Tell them what the Messiah means to you, and why you believe that Jesus is the Messiah," it said with command.

I continued my private conversation.

"Lord," I said, "if this is you, I must ask if you know what you're doing? You know these people don't believe in you and, besides, you know Dr. Monroe's orders."

I waited for an answer. Nothing came.

"Well, Lord, if this is really you speaking to me, you'll have to literally make me speak. I don't want this beautiful relationship with these people to be ruined by me."

Just as the professor next to me finished speaking, my mouth just popped open.

"Ma'am," I said, "you have shared what the Messiah means to you. I'd like to share with you what the Messiah means to me, and why I believe that Jesus is the Messiah."

The room grew so silent I could hear my own heart beating. *The room grew totally silent.* Everybody was looking at me. Dr. Monroe actually turned pale.

"One year ago today, my son died," I began.

I told the story of Jeff's vision and how Jesus had been so real to my son, quoting Scriptures the Lord gave me.

As I was yet speaking, the professor next to me grabbed my arm and said, "Excuse me, but I must go. My wife is waiting for me."

He left the room abruptly. At the same time people began moving around and talking.

"Oh, oh," I thought. "I really blew it." It hadn't been the Lord talking to me, but Satan. Even Rick deserted me, going out on the balcony to get some air.

I didn't know what to do. I just thought to myself, "You and your big mouth! You really blew it this time."

All of a sudden a woman from back in the corner of the room came over to me. She sat down on the stool Rick had vacated.

"Where *do* you get your strength?" she asked. "You are a remarkable woman."

Her voice rising, she asked me how I could believe in God when young Israeli soldiers were dying, and terrorists were doing their deadly work.

"I lost my son two years ago," she said, near tears. "I prayed for his life. If there was a God, He would have let my son live. He would have let your son live. My son was only seven." She started crying.

"What is your name?" I asked. She was an attractive young woman, about my age.

"Yael," she answered.

"Yael," I said, "God loves you and sees your bitterness and your sorrow. The peace you see in me only Jesus can give. I believe Jesus wants you to have the same peace. My strength isn't my own; it comes from my Lord."

154

As I continued to share the gospel and the many mighty works of God, the dean, who had brought us to his home, walked over and sat down to listen to what I was telling Yael.

"I believe Jesus is here tonight, Yael, waiting to give you this same peace you see in me," I said. "Will you let me pray with you?"

"Yes," she said without any hesitation.

We prayed together. The others had left and were scattered around the room, ignoring us.

She began to cry and I could see our Lord ministering to all the hurt she had bottled up inside her. I asked if she would like to accept Jesus as her Messiah, her Savior.

"Yes," she said, as she wiped away a tear trickling down her cheek. We—including the dean—bowed our heads, and Yael asked the Lord to forgive her of her sins, and invited Jesus into her life, and accepted him as her Messiah. She continued to weep as we finished praying. Then her face became radiant as the sun, and peace shone from her eyes. I knew she had found Christ. Our Lord's peace had taken hold of her.

I asked how she had lost her son.

"It was a very rare heart disease," she said. "There are only a few cases like it in the world."

My heart missed a beat.

"Yael, what is the name of the disease that killed your son?" I said quietly.

"Myocardiopathy," she said.

"Yael, Yael," I said gently, "do you realize what has happened this evening? This meeting was not by accident. God planned our meeting. My family died of the same disease that claimed your son."

Only nineteen cases of myocardiopathy had been

reported in the history of the world. God had miraculously brought us together.

The professor who had left the room returned. He stopped in front of me. He looked down at me, took my hands in his, and raised me up to him.

"I didn't want to leave without telling you something," he said. Tears began running down his cheeks. "I didn't leave to be rude or to deliberately interrupt your story. My heart was pounding so badly that—" He had to stop.

"I am a rabbi," he continued. "I didn't want to lose my emotions and break down in front of all of these people. I want you to know I believe that what your son saw is true."

Before he left, he told me, "I have something to consider now. This Messiah you speak about. I will tell my students about him."

I hugged him and told him that I loved him with the love Christ had given me.

"I believe you," he said. "God has given you much love to share."

We returned to our hotel, our hearts soaring with joy. A late dinner was waiting for us and we strolled into the dining room to a scrumptious Israeli meal. Amos, our bus driver, whom I had been witnessing to all through the trip, came and sat between Rick and me.

"Betty, that was some story you shared tonight," he said. "All these days I have spent with you, I would never guess you had just gone through an ordeal with your family as you have. And your son's vision is something I've never heard before. Being so young, he had no reason to make such a story up, being so sick and all."

"No, he didn't, Amos," I replied. "And the way you

see me is only through the grace of our Lord. It is only obtainable through Christ Jesus, the Messiah."

"After dinner, could you tell me more about what the Bible has to say about Jesus being our Messiah? Will you show me where in the Bible that it prophesied Him to be the Messiah?" he asked.

We invited Amos to our room after dinner and shared with him the prophecies in Isaiah and Jeremiah concerning the Messiah. We gave him a New Testament written in Hebrew that Doctor Monroe had given us. We read together in John about our Savior. He was astonished when he read about the woman at the well, and the answer Jesus gave to her when she said to him, "I know that the Messiah comes, which is called Christ: when he does come, he will tell us all things." Jesus said to her, "*I* that speak to you am He" (John 4:25-26 paraphrased).

A look of amazement came over him. Then he said, "I want to go to my room and read more alone with myself."

"May we pray for you that the Lord will reveal himself to you through these Scriptures you will read?" I asked.

"Yes," he answered.

A few days later, we were at a hotel operated by Arabs. We were sitting around a table singing songs in Hebrew we had learned at school, when two Arab-Moslem boys came and sat down to join us. Amos was there too.

The Arabs asked us what we were singing about. We told them we were singing about Jesus. They acknowledged their belief of Jesus being the Messiah, but they could not understand the virgin birth, which would make Him God.

157

As we opened our Bibles to the verses, and began to present our evidence to the event of the virgin birth, Amos began to minister unbelievably to this fact and that Christ is the Messiah. We were all stunned.

When he realized what he was saying, and the power behind what he was relating, he stopped abruptly and began to cry.

Through his sobbing words, he said, "What am I saying? Here I am, a Jew, telling a Moslem about the virgin birth of Christ."

Two days later, we went to the airport to return home. Many Israelis and Arabs had learned about Christ through us and through hearing the story of Jeff's vision.

As the plane was taxiing out to the runway, the seat next to me was empty. I had planned to stretch out for the long trip home. All of a sudden a young Israeli, carrying an overnight bag, plopped into the seat next to me. I thought, "Where did he come from?"

We were excitedly talking about the successes we had shared and I guess our enthusiasm spilled over into the lap of the stranger.

In a heavily accented voice, he said, "Why are you so happy? And why do you love Israel so much?"

"Because we're Biblical Zionists," I said, smiling. "We believe Israel is God's chosen people, and through them he sent the Messiah to save us from our sins. Jews and Gentiles alike."

The plane was cruising comfortably at 35,000 feet. He stared at me.

"You believe that there is a God?" he asked, almost incredulously.

"Yes, I believe there is a God," I answered. "Do you?"

"There is a God all right," he said thoughtfully. "He

is in the trees, in the flowers, and in the hills, but I do not believe in a personal God."

My Bible was beneath my seat. I picked it up and asked him if he believed in the Bible. He admitted that he didn't know if the Bible was true or not.

"Let me show you through the Bible that God is a real person."

He shrugged. We went through parts of Genesis, and I quoted Scripture, showing that God walked in the garden.

"If he walked and talked, He has to be a person, right?" I said. He nodded. We went from Genesis to Revelation. Every time I came across a verse that showed God as a person, I pointed it out to him.

He admitted he had never read such words before.

I shared with him the story of Christ dying on the cross. He admitted having heard the story, but said he wasn't sure whether Christ was actually the Messiah. The Lord quickened my heart to tell him the story of my son's vision.

When I was finished, he said, "Don't ask me to explain it, but I believe you. I believe what your son saw is true."

Incredibly, he told me that he wanted to be a Christian. The Holy Spirit was working overtime at 35,000 feet. We prayed with two other members of our group joining in. He knelt in the aisle and accepted Christ as his Messiah.

We gave him a Bible written in Hebrew so he could study God's words more clearly. He had never seen a Bible in Hebrew before and was grateful for the gift. All the way to London, he didn't lay that Bible down. I knew the Lord was teaching him His truths. I thought back to when I first read my Bible, and the hours I spent in it.

In London I told Dr. Monroe what had happened. He grinned.

"I know," he said. "I saw all of it. Do you know who your new convert is? He's just a member of the Israeli Air Security, that's all. While you were preaching the gospel to him, he was supposed to be watching out for hijackers!"

We had a twenty-minute wait before boarding for our flight to New York. I took a seat on the plane, and, again, the seat next to me was unoccupied. As the plane began rolling down the runway, a young man carrying the same kind of suitcase as my earlier convert plopped into the seat next to me. I exchanged glances with Dr. Monroe. He rolled his eyes. I realized he was Air Security. A little frightened, I decided to keep my mouth shut. It was dark and I tried to sleep, but I was miserable. I thought, "Maybe the other security told him about me and he's planning to put me under arrest for preaching the gospel."

Nothing happened. About an hour and a half out of New York, a stewardess woke us to serve us breakfast. I began chatting with my seatmate, choosing my words with care. When he asked what had prompted my trip to Israel, I thought, "Here it goes again, Lord!" I explained to him as I did the last fellow about our being Biblical Zionists and our belief in the Messiah.

"Oh, you're a Christian," he said.

"Yes, and you're Jewish, aren't you?" I replied.

"No," he declared. "I live in Israel, but I'm not Jewish. Jewish is a religion. I don't believe in the Jewish religion."

He had studied the Bible in school and said he believed in God. That perked my interest.

"Do you believe Jesus is the Messiah?" I persisted.

"No. Jesus was a great prophet. He was a great teacher, but I don't believe he was the Messiah."

Out came my Bible. I asked him if he had ever read the New Testament, and he admitted he hadn't. He believed all of the Old Testament, including the book of Isaiah. I took him through Isaiah and shared with him the verses Isaiah had written about the coming of the Messiah. Then we went to Psalms and Jeremiah, and I showed him the prophecies. When I was convinced I had him hooked, I took him into the New Testament and read to him about the fulfillment of the prophecies.

He seemed genuinely amazed at the tie-in between the Old and New Testaments.

"Can I share a story with you?" I asked.

"Sure," he responded.

Again, I shared Jeff's vision with an Israeli, and yes, you guessed it. Jesus had another convert.

On the flight from New York to Dallas, we were all quite tired from the long flight across the ocean. Everyone was resting and it was very quiet. I lay back in my seat and thought of all the wonderful works the Lord had done through us in Israel.

As I was pondering them in my mind, the Lord spoke to my heart.

"You said I had no ministry for you, that I didn't send you to Bible school. I have showed you through these lives the mighty power of salvation. I have showed you I have called you to the ministry and I am able to use you for my glory. Remember, even out of death comes life."

161

Epilogue

This testimony has no ending, only a beginning. This is so because that is the way it is in the kingdom of God.

The sorrow, grief and pain I experienced in my life were for the purpose of cultivating my character and molding me to reflect Christ-like qualities. They also served to give me the ability of being able to understand and comfort others facing similar trials in their own lives.

I can now understand why Peter said, "You should be exceedingly glad on this account, though now for a little while you may be distressed by trials, and suffer temptations, so that the genuineness of your faith may be tested which is infinitely more precious than perishable gold" (1 Peter 1:6-7 paraphrased), and why Paul could say, "Rejoice in suffering" through manifold temptations. The positive end of these burdens and afflictions blossoms into praise, rejoicing, and gratitude to Christ.

When it seems that the agony will last forever, be assured that weeping only lasts for a night. The dawn is just about to break. Just as our Master promised sunshine after the rain, we know that joy surely comes in the morning.

Faith and wisdom comes in trusting and depending on God, and not questioning, "Lord, why me?" He alone sits in authority over every situation. I know He is in control. In Christ I see the Resurrection. When we come to the crossroads of life, we can understand, we can look, gather and appropriate from the One we know, the Lord Jesus Christ. He will give us the Way— and the Truth, and the Life. God desires us not to be conquered, but that we be the overcomers.

As I take a moment to pause and reflect over these past years, I can, and do, praise Him for everything.

If I was placed in a time tunnel and sent back to that span of my life, fully conscious of those events, I would go into it unflinchingly and relive that period over again. I would go because I would see the results of an undying faith in an awesome, sovereign Father and His glorified Son. I would also envision the multiplied spiritual family He would grant me as I shared the peace our loving and compassionate God has given me. He has granted to the world unlimited grace through His Son, and through Him, repentance and forgiveness are available. And because of His resurrection, we also share in that resurrection into eternal life.

Note:
    If the reader would like to send comments, receive counseling, or inquire about speaking engagements, he can write the author at the following address:

Rev. Elizabeth Gardner
Fountain of Life Ministry
P.O. Box 39073
Phoenix, Arizona 85069

Appendix

Cardiomyopathy is the name given to a group of diseases that cause damage to the heart muscle. This was recognized in alcoholic drinkers as early as 1880 in Germany. A clear understanding of the entity was independently made by Dr. Mattingly and Dr. Brigden in 1958. Since then, many people have contributed to the understanding of the disease; but in spite of many scientific contributions in the last two decades, our knowledge about this is still limited.

Although the word "cardiomyopathy" may apply to all cases in which the heart muscle is involved, it is now commonly used to identify a group of conditions where there is no apparent cause for the heart muscle involvement.

This condition affects both males and females and may be familial or nonfamilial. In some cases it may be due to a virus infection; however, even in those not due to virus the condition may surface following a flu or an upper respiratory infection.

Usually, the disease primarily involves the heart,

and this malfunction ultimately causes impairment of other organs. We do not know the exact mechanism by which the heart muscle becomes involved, but we do know that the involved muscle shows total disturbance in its energy metabolism and as a result is unable to contract properly. It is also incapable of transferring fatty acids into energy compounds. This involves the destruction of the mitochondria in some cases. Beyond this, we have not been able to understand why these ultra-microscopic structures of the heart muscle cell are selectively destroyed.

There are three types of primary myocardiopathy, namely: congestive, restrictive and hypertrophic. Among these three, the congestive cardiomyopathy is the most common and is usually nonfamilial. However, in the case of Mrs. Gardner's children and her first husband, it was a familial type of congestive cardiomyopathy and there is but one—or possibly two—reports of this in medical literature. It is usually precipitated by flu or upper respiratory infection. The heart starts enlarging and is unable to contract and pump the blood, resulting in fluid retention in the liver and the legs. Finally, the kidneys start failing, and ultimately death results. The time between the onset of the symptoms and death varies in different people. It may be extremely fast, as in Frank's and the children's cases, or may be slow and take years as in others. In the restrictive type, the heart cannot dilate at all, because it is very stiff; heart failure and death result. In the hypertrophic type, the muscles of the heart are so thick that they reduce the cavity inside, and this leads ultimately to heart failure or arrhythmia, resulting in death.

Although many advances have been made in treating these patients and helping them to have a comfortable life as long as they live, we have not yet been able to find a cure, short of replacement with a new heart. Even in some of these cases where heart transplants have been done, the new heart again becomes involved in the same kind of process. Therefore, at present, we are unable to predict what the future will be. However, we do hope with the new drugs being developed and with better understanding of the ultra-structure of the heart muscles and their mechanism of action, we may in the future be able to find the cause of this myopathy and may be able to attack the problem at that level and help either in curing or in preventing this disease.

T.N. Seshagiri